WOMEN
REMEMBER
THE WAR
1941 – 1945

★

MICHAEL E. STEVENS
Editor

ELLEN D. GOLDLUST
Assistant Editor

Center for Documentary History
STATE HISTORICAL SOCIETY OF WISCONSIN
Madison: 1993

Wisconsin Women in World War II
Oral History Project Interviewers

Kristina Ackley

Kathryn Borkowski

Tracey Deutsch

Stephen Kolman

LIBRARY OF CONGRESS CATALOGING-IN-PUBLICATION DATA
Women Remember the War, 1941–1945. (Voices of the Wisconsin Past.)
Michael E. Stevens, editor. Ellen D. Goldlust, assistant editor.
Includes bibliographical references and index.
ISBN 0-87020-272-3 (pbk.)
1. World War, 1939–1945—Women—Wisconsin—Interviews
2. World War, 1939–1945—Personal narratives, American.
3. Oral History.
I. Stevens, Michael E. II. Goldlust, Ellen D. III. State Historical Society of
Wisconsin. IV. Series.
D810.W7W67   1993
940.53′ 15042—dc20
                                                          93-23197
                                                          CIP

Contents

Preface

"I think I became a most self-sufficient person. I know that I had to do a lot of things that I would not maybe have done had there been a man around the house."

— Rose Kaminski

LIKE millions of other Wisconsin women, Rose Kaminski's life changed because of World War II. Living in Milwaukee with her young daughter while her husband served in the U.S. Navy, Kaminski worked as a crane operator in a local defense plant. She made do with rationing, tried to balance her roles as mother and breadwinner, worried about her husband, and rushed to his side after receiving a telegram informing her that he had been wounded in a training accident. Kaminski and others like her saw nothing remarkable about their lives in wartime. They did their work quietly, making sure that life continued with as little disruption as possible, but their efforts wrought important changes in American life.

Despite the wide variety of paths followed by women during World War II, the popular view of women during that time often remains as narrow as the outdated histories that excluded women altogether. Having rediscovered "Rosie the Riveter," we tend to forget the many other roles played by women. Yet uncovering the varied texture of the daily lives of Wisconsin women during the war can be a daunting experience because of the relative absence of sources.

Women Remember the War offers a brief introduction to the experiences of Wisconsin women in World War II as told in their own words. This volume includes selections from oral history interviews in which women addressed issues concerning their wartime lives. It is the second in the *Voices of the Wisconsin Past* series, which presents accounts of the state's history from the vantage point of the participants. The series centers on the ordinary citizens of the state and offers accounts unmediated by the historian's narrative. *Women Remember the War* provides a rich mix of insights, incorporating the perspectives of workers in factories, in offices, and on farms as well as those of wives and mothers who found their work in the home. This book illustrates the varied experiences of women during a crucial era in our history.

With more than 300,000 Wisconsin men in uniform (out of a male population of 1.6 million), women's responsibilities on the home front increased. The absence of so many men and the increased demands of war production led to patriotic calls for women to supply the needed labor. As elsewhere, Wisconsin women responded to the call.

World War II changed the composition of the work force, but it did not introduce the idea of paid labor to Wisconsin women. In 1940, about one in five Wisconsin women over the age of fourteen worked for wages. If employment patterns in Wisconsin followed national trends, that number probably increased to one in three by 1944. The war, although resulting in substantial growth in women's paid employment, accelerated a trend that began before and continued after the war.

More significantly, the war redistributed women into new occupations. More women took jobs in industrial settings than ever before, although the field remained male-dominated. Female access to other occupations changed during the war. Before the war, for example, clerical positions were equally divided between men and women; by 1945, women dominated this field.

The war also provided new opportunities for women in the military. Women had long served as nurses, but the war allowed them finally to achieve equal pay and full military rank. Shortages of men for combat roles led to the creation of women's units in all branches of the military, and nearly 8,000 Wisconsin women served in this capacity. Because these units served primarily stateside, a number of women who wanted to go overseas but who could not qualify as nurses joined the Red Cross and worked in Europe, Africa, the Pacific, and Asia.

Despite increased opportunities for women in the marketplace, domestic roles remained vital during the war. The marriage rate jumped 28 percent between 1939 and 1942, in part because the improved economy permitted marriages that had been delayed because of the Great Depression and in part because of weddings that had been hurried as a result of the war. The birthrate also increased from the lows of the depression era, although it did not achieve the high rates of the postwar "baby boom" years. And despite efforts to increase female participation in paid employment, most married women continued in traditional roles, as fewer than one in four wives worked for wages in 1944. The overwhelming majority of mothers with young children rejected wage work, with fewer than one in eight women with children under the age of ten in the workplace.

*   *   *   *   *

We could not tell women's stories of the war in their own words by relying exclusively on conventional documentary material. Relative to those of male veterans, few Wisconsin women's letters from the World War II era have been donated to archival repositories, and those letters that have been preserved frequently came from women who served in the military rather than from the great majority who did their work on the home front. In addition, information on domestic issues often remains underdocumented in surviving correspondence and has to be teased out of alternate sources.

To remedy this flaw, the State Historical Society of Wisconsin launched an oral history project to document the history of Wisconsin women during World War II. The project sought to illustrate the diversity of women's experience rather than to create a statistically accurate profile of Wisconsin women. In addition to covering the role of women in the public arena, the interviews put special emphasis on personal issues, such as dating, family life, and child care, that conventional accounts often overlook.

The project's oral history collection contains hundreds of hours of tape representing interviews with more than a hundred Wisconsin women. It is available in the form of transcripts or on tape at the Society's archives. This book represents only a sampling from that collection, and it touches on the major themes found in the interviews. Because the interviews took place fifty years after the war with women ranging in age from their mid-sixties to their early nineties, it necessarily deals with the history of women in their childbearing years who started or hoped to start marriages, families, or jobs during wartime. Those whose stories appear here ranged in age from fourteen to thirty-nine at the opening of the war, with fully half in their twenties. (In 1940 more than 40 percent of the state's nearly 1.5 million females were between the ages of fifteen and thirty-nine, and another 25 percent were under fifteen.)

The oral histories in this volume share the same drawbacks and benefits as others of this genre of historical documentation. Subsequent experiences filter and affect memories of the past, because all of these women know how their personal as well as the global stories turned out. They no longer are in doubt about whether their loved ones would return, when or how the war would end, or whether they would keep their jobs after the war.

Conversely, the oral history interviews provide documentation that would otherwise be lost. In addition, they provided these women with the opportunity to reflect on the changes wrought in their lives and their society because of the war. They became, in effect, not only subjects for the historian's examination but interpreters of their own lives and times. When Rose Kaminski says, "I think I became a most self-sufficient person," she offers her considered evaluation of how the war changed her and others' lives. She becomes, for the moment, her own historian.

The interviews have been arranged topically, although they overlap to some degree because life does not neatly divide into separate subjects. The initial two chapters explore women's experiences in the labor force. The first chapter deals with mothers who worked in industrial settings. The second chapter looks at the experiences of young, single women working largely in white-collar professions. These women recall not only their work experiences but also the environment in which they met young men and dating customs during the wartime shortage of eligible young men. Chapter 3 presents interviews with women who either worked as military nurses or joined women's branches of the military, as well as interviews with Red Cross workers who served in the Pacific theater.

Chapter 4 contains accounts by women who cared for young children in the home. These women address issues of childbearing and child rearing as well as a variety of other subjects, including volunteer work, rationing, and women's networks. Chapter 5 deals with high school girls, whose adolescent years were marked by the upheaval of the war, an often overlooked area.

Finally, women also coped with the anxiety of seeing their sons, brothers, husbands, and boyfriends join the military. Chapter 6 contains interviews with several women who talk about how they coped with the possibility of loss. The book concludes with a chapter about women's reactions to the news of V-E Day and V-J Day and with an epilogue in which the interviewees speculate on how the war changed their lives.

More than 8,000 Wisconsin men died in the war, but this volume does not contain any extended comments from women about losing a loved one. Questions on the subject elicited strong emotions from many women as well as requests to turn the tape recorder off. Their relative silence speaks eloquently of how deeply the pain of war still cuts a half a century later.

*   *   *   *   *

The transcripts of oral interviews conducted during 1992 and 1993 form the basis of the text printed here. We have tried to create a clean, readable text without sacrificing the original language of the interviews. Because written English differs from spoken English, we employed a number of conventions to deal with variations. We did not add or change any words, and we did not tamper with grammar or sentence structure. Words added to clarify the text always appear in brackets. The transcripts omit false starts as well as filler words, such as "you know" or "um." We made no attempt to preserve dialect or pronunciation. The original tapes are available for those interested in such nuances.

The interviews ranged in length from one hour to more than three hours, and the texts presented here are excerpts. Questions and answers are presented in the order in which they occurred. When part of the answer to a question has been deleted, we note it with ellipsis points, although we have not used them to indicate omissions of entire questions and answers. The questions asked by the interviewers appear in italic type and have been edited for clarity.

In every case, we contacted the interviewees and asked them to review the text selected for inclusion in this book. In several cases they requested (and we made) minor changes that correct inaccuracies or clarify statements.

*   *   *   *   *

This volume would not be possible without the generosity of the women who agreed to let us print excerpts from their interviews and who generously donated photographs and other documentary material. We gratefully acknowledge them for allowing us to present their stories.

Kathy Borkowski and Steve Kolman have been involved with the Wisconsin Women during World War II Oral History Project from the very beginning and have conducted the great majority of the interviews contained in the book. Tina Ackley worked with the project as an intern in the summer of 1992, and two of the interviews that she conducted are excerpted here. Her recordings of the wartime recollections of sixteen Native American women have added immeasurably to the value of the oral history collection. Tracey Deutsch joined the project at a later stage and conducted several interviews that took place too late for inclusion in the book. The project staff has tolerated equipment malfunctions, conducted field trips in Wisconsin's frigid winters, and borne with scheduling mishaps with good cheer. The interviewers' creativity and ingenuity have been essential to the success of the project.

We also would like to thank Charmaine Harbort and Lisa Harris, who labored long and hard transcribing the interviews. Paul Hass's editorial pen again proved vital in our efforts to turn our manuscript into a book. H. Nicholas Muller III, Robert Thomasgard, and Peter Gottlieb continued to provide the support necessary to continue the *Voices* series.

*   *   *   *   *

The State Historical Society has been working to preserve the record of Wisconsin's history since 1846. Volumes in the *Voices of the Wisconsin Past* series would not have been possible without the donation of materials relating to the state's history. The Society continues to collect letters, diaries, and other documentary material. The Society invites persons wishing to discuss the donation of manuscript material to contact the Archives, State Historical Society of Wisconsin, 816 State Street, Madison, WI 53706.

WOMEN REMEMBER THE WAR
1941 – 1945

Prologue

DECEMBER 7, 1941, was cool yet pleasant in most of Wisconsin. After attending church services in the morning, many families sat down to Sunday dinner and looked forward to an afternoon of relaxation before returning to work the next morning. In Milwaukee, people strolled down Wisconsin Avenue, looking at Christmas displays in the shop windows. Tavern owners around the state tuned their radios to broadcasts of the Chicago Bears–Chicago Cardinals football game.

By mid-afternoon, ominous rumors began to spread. Those listening to the radio heard news bulletins about the Japanese attack on Pearl Harbor as early as 1:25 P.M. Moviegoers had their afternoon matinees interrupted by news reports. Many remained in their seats in stunned silence as the film flickered back on the screen; others left for home to turn on the radio. By 5:00 P.M., newspapers began to hit the streets with extra editions containing blazing headlines.

Although diplomatic relations with Japan been deteriorating for months, the turn of events stunned many people. Local telephone companies called in extra operators to deal with jammed phone lines. In Manitowoc, the shipyards tightened their security because of fear of sabotage. Newspaper reporters set out to obtain local reaction. Marian Anderson, a student at the University of Wisconsin, told a *Capital Times* reporter, "I'm mad — good and mad — and want to find something a girl can do to help win the war." Those with radios stayed nearby to hear updates; those without clustered in restaurants, bars, and drugstores where they could hear the news and share their anxiety with others.

Attention continued to focus on war news the next day. Army recruiting stations did heavy business. Many Wisconsin residents tuned in their radios at eleven the next morning to hear President Roosevelt's "day of infamy" speech before a joint session of Congress. The University of Wisconsin excused students from classes to hear the speech.

Where were you when you heard about Pearl Harbor? The news of the Japanese attack remains vividly fixed in minds of nearly everyone who lived through that era. The events of that day would change their lives.

Irene Kruck (Manitowoc)
My husband worked at the local newspaper, and he called and told me to turn on the radio, and I turned on the radio and I heard about Pearl Harbor. As soon as I heard it, I thought, "Pearl Harbor, explosion" — then I began to pray. That was the first thing I did. Then after that I thought, "I wonder how long this will last." I wonder if my sons, especially the one that was beginning his high school, would have to serve in the army or if he'd be called or what effect it would have on my family. I had brothers and many good friends. So many things go through your mind that you're just in sort of a daze.

Mary Joan Pinard (Prairie du Chien)
A number of my classmates and friends, we had just graduated in June of 1941, and we were gathering together at a place called Kabers. It was a restaurant/bar type of thing and we used to get together on Sunday afternoons and just sit and have a cup of coffee or a glass of beer and shoot the breeze. And we were all sitting there together when somebody came in rather ashen-looking and said, "Pearl Harbor's just been bombed." We immediately assumed, of course, that it was a very poor joke. We were well aware some people had already been drafted from the area and there had been talk of enlistment by different ones but we knew something was coming, but we still didn't anticipate something like that. It was a very sobering afternoon. We all sat together and talked about what we thought were the possibilities ahead. It was an aging day. I'm a little teary because two of the young men that were with us that afternoon did not come back. We grew up fast — we were all seventeen, eighteen at the time.

Luida Sanders (Wittenberg)
I was at church . . . and the church had been remodeled and we were dedicating the new sanctuary that day. I was in the choir and sitting up in the front. One of the men who ordinarily would have been there had been home feeling sick, and he heard the radio, and he came dashing over and called the minister out. Then they made the announcement, and so from dedication it went into a prayer service.

Loa Fergot (Neenah)
We'd been to church and had dinner, and I think we were just sitting around the table when we heard about it. And my mother started to cry, and I remember thinking, "Well, it's terrible, but why is she crying?" You know, I really couldn't understand that. And of course, I had a brother who was a senior at Lawrence [College, in Appleton,] then, and so I'm sure she was thinking about him immediately. But that's where I first heard about it. And that night [we went to hear] the "Messiah" at Lawrence, . . . and that was probably one of the most meaningful concerts I've ever attended, if not the most. The place was packed — and it was almost as though everybody in it was kind of stunned or something, just kind of sitting in shock. . . . "Why do the nations so fiercely rage together" — the bass who sang that was just tremendous. He was really great, and after he got through with it, it was just complete quiet, and people were — everybody was crying. Makes me want to cry now, to think of it.

Jean Lechnir (Prairie du Chien)
My husband and I were visiting my father and stepmother in Minneapolis and we had my six-month-old daughter with us because we took her up there to show her off, and that's where we heard about it. The feeling, well, you know when you have your heart in your mouth, well, mine went right down to my toes because I had a funny feeling right then that my husband was going to be involved in spite of the fact that we had a baby. We didn't know how and it just put a damper on the whole party you might say, and we came home feeling very low but very angry, very angry.

Joyce Westerman (Kenosha)
We lived on a farm, . . . and it didn't have any water or electricity. And we had a big potbellied stove to heat the house. Well, at that point, we were standing around the potbellied stove, with two young men that often came to visit us — we worked for his parents — and we were just conversing and heard it over the radio. And this one young man, Everett, said, "Well, I guess I'll be gone tomorrow." And at that point, the next day, he was gone to the service. And as it turned out he came home once while he was training — his father had passed away — and then he went to the war, and went through almost the whole war, and was killed near the end of the war.

Lucy Veltri (Racine)
I recall being at the Granada Theater in Racine, Wisconsin, and it was about six blocks away from my home. I was thirteen years old at the time, and I recall the theater becoming dark. They turned off the movie and then the owner/manager of the theater went up on stage — the lights went up on stage in front of the curtains — and he announced that Japan had bombed Pearl Harbor, and I was scared to death. It frightened me so much. I don't remember what else he said. And he got off stage and the movie went back on, and I was amazed because I thought, "They're going to be here any minute — how can anybody look at the movie?" In fact, it frightened me so much that I can't remember what the movie was. I ran all the way home. No one was home, but three doors away my cousin lived there, and the relatives were there because they were having a birthday over there. So I went over there, and all the relatives were crying, all the women. One in particular had ten children, and six of them were boys, and most of them were ready to be called into service. So she thought they're all going to leave and they're not going to come back, and she was just so upset. Everybody was crying with her and it was terrible. It was just awful.

Dorothy Weingrod (Milwaukee)
I was home, and we had actually planned a party that evening for a very good friend of ours who was going into the service because his number had come up in the draft. . . . [The draft had existed since 1940, but] the whole tenor of the evening changed because all of a sudden we were in the war and it was an entirely different feeling about his leaving. There was much more stress and much more worry. He was the first one that was actually going into the service. So it was a traumatic day. . . . Being Jewish, of course, I felt that this was something that was very important. We should have gone in, and we should have gotten in even sooner, but war is a frightening thing.

Frieda Schurch (Barneveld)
In those days . . . the Swiss Reform church met in the afternoon because they rented the church, and we were about to leave for church, my dad and I, when my brother told us that [Pearl Harbor had been attacked] — he was listening to the radio. And then we went to church and the minister gave a prayer thanking God that we still weren't in the war. And I did not have the courage to tell anybody after the service that Pearl Harbor had begun and we had been attacked, and my dad didn't either. And nobody else was talk-

ing about it, so we had a feeling we were probably the only two
[who knew] because we were about the last ones to church. But we
knew a big change was coming.

1

Winning the War in the Factories

ROSIE THE RIVETER endures among the most vivid images of women in World War II. She helped the war effort by working on the factory floor in a defense plant, replacing a man who had gone to fight and losing none of her femininity in the process — or so the story goes. Although women made remarkable contributions in industrial settings, the truth remains far more complicated than this simple image.

In 1940, more than 260,000 out of nearly 1.2 million Wisconsin women over the age of fourteen worked for wages. With wartime labor shortages, many women moved into the work force, and by 1944 approximately 400,000 Wisconsin women had obtained paid employment. Nationwide, two of every ten working women found employment in factories before the war; by 1944, that number increased to three in ten as women responded to patriotic appeals to aid the war effort by taking jobs for which they previously were not considered. Even with the great influx of women into manufacturing, however, the vast majority remained in more traditional clerical and service jobs, and the number of women employed in those fields grew dramatically as well. Although only a small minority of all American women found themselves in industrial settings for the first time, their importance lies in the way that they challenged established stereotypes and served as models for later generations of women.

The 12 percent of American women with children under ten who worked outside the home in 1944 faced additional burdens. Whether or not their husbands served in the military, these women still shouldered much of the burden of maintaining the household and caring for the children. Furthermore, the war made these tasks more difficult: rationing and the shortage of consumer goods made shopping for basic household commodities more difficult, and

"I've found the job where I fit best!"

FIND YOUR WAR JOB
In Industry–Agriculture–Business

A 1943 poster produced by the U.S. Office of War Information urging women to contribute to war production.

many stores had closed by the time workers finished their shifts. Although the government and employers tried to establish child-care facilities, most women wage workers rejected them in favor of more informal arrangements.

The defense industry played a prominent role in Wisconsin during the war. Shipbuilding became a major industry in Manitowoc and Superior, and numerous large companies, including the West Bend Aluminum Company, Allis-Chalmers, Allen-Bradley, Rayovac, and J. I. Case, received government contracts and converted from their usual products to defense work. Rose Kaminski and Evelyn Gotzion are two of the women who obtained nontraditional jobs, and their stories offer accounts of how they balanced their outside jobs with their family responsibilities.

Rose Kaminski

Born to Polish immigrants in Kenosha in 1918, Rose (Gudynowski) Kaminski moved to Milwaukee at age ten. She married John Kaminski in 1937 and has two daughters, one born in 1941 and the second in 1948. Her husband was drafted in early 1944 and served on a minesweeper in the navy. Beginning in early 1943, she worked in the machine shop of the General Electric Supercharger plant. After about four months there, she became a crane operator for the Rex Chain Belt Company, and in February, 1944, she obtained a similar position with Harnischfeger Corporation, remaining there until March, 1946, when she was released from her job to accommodate a returning veteran. She returned to Harnischfeger in 1950, working there until she retired in February, 1981. Widowed in November, 1988, Rose Kaminski still lives on Milwaukee's south side.

I didn't work [at the supercharger plant] very long, and the thing I remember the most about it is that we replaced the men at that time. We ran a machine shop, and men came in and set up the machines, and we were like little robots. We just picked up the pieces and then inserted pieces in the milling machines and in the presses and in the threading machines and counted them and put them in bins. You really felt like a machine, working a machine. It was not really fulfilling in the sense that you were really doing something or accomplishing something, because whenever you needed anything, a man had to come over and do it, because you did not know the ins and outs. Even though we were sent to night school for a while, that was just a short time. . . . And then they were asking for women to volunteer and they were hiring at what is now Rexnord, the old Rex Chain Belt Company, and they had an ordnance plant. . . .

One of the women in the neighborhood was taking care of children for mothers that were [working], and she was up in her years. I would say she was about sixty-five — an old grandmother — a little German woman who was just wonderful. She had about three children. Would you call it a day-care center now? But the beautiful part of it is, she had a fenced-in yard and she took care of these children and she was wonderful. She taught them their ABCs and their numbers and she taught them little songs and the kids would dress up in clothes and take a flag and parade around the neighborhood. Even they knew there was a war on. It was really funny.

This is where my daughter stayed. I don't think I would have gone into any work had I not been able to leave her with somebody as fine as this women was. She devoted her time just to the children and in her old German brogue she always used to say, "I know that I am needed." And it was wonderful for this little old lady to do this. (I say little old lady, and here I am already the age that this little old lady was. I have to watch myself!)

So, anyway, back to Chain Belt. I went in to apply for work as an inspector. I thought, "Oh well, this is going to be a little bit more meaningful: inspection work. I won't be a robot." We went in there — there was quite a few of us — and we went into the factory, and we were all in the shop area, and this gentlemen came up and said, "Well, we're going to be hiring inspectors, and we're also going to be needing several crane operators." And my ears perked up right away because my stepfather was a crane operator for years, and I always heard about it but never knew what it was. I was not familiar with the shop positions. I said to him, "Oh, I'd like to see what a crane looks like and what I'd have to do. I'd really be interested because my dad was a crane operator." And he said, "Fine, we'll show you what you'd have to do." So he took several of us and walked into the factory, and here was this great big ordnance plant with machines all lined up in rows and everything and great big gun barrels. They were making great big howitzer barrels for the guns. Overhead were the cranes, and he showed us what we'd have to do.

I thought, "Oh, is that what my father used to do?" I said, "I'd like to try and see if I could do it." He said, "Well, you just have to learn how to work the crane, and all you'd have to do is pick up these great big" — they're like grinders that would go in and thread the barrels of these big howitzers — "and you'd have to set them in and then you'd just have to sit and wait until all of this goes through a procedure before you would take and lift up this part and move the gun barrel onto a flatcar and it would go out." I thought, "Well, gee, that sounded pretty nice." He said, "We'll train you. It will take you three weeks and you'll be able to run a crane yourself." Well, I was running one in three days. It just came to me; I loved it. There was no problem. It was not difficult, and here I thought, "You can see the gun barrels. You know that it's part of the war." It wasn't like at the other place where you had piddly little pieces, and you didn't know where it belonged. This seemed like part of it. You were doing something. You were accomplishing something. Well, they closed the [ordnance] plant within about six to eight months. I don't think I worked there a year. There were several of us ladies that, now, where are we going to go and what are we going to do? I don't know if you're aware of the Harnischfeger plant. They make the huge overhead cranes themselves and [also] made excavating machines, so we decided we would go over there and try getting a job there. I want you to know that we were being paid eighty cents an hour.

Was that amount comparable to what the men were making during the time, or did you have a sense that there was a difference?

I think there was a difference, but not a radical difference, because when you stop to think that when we worked at the supercharger plant you don't expect a machinist to come in and set up a machine and have you run it and take advantage of all their knowledge and experience. You were just performing a part of their job that would give them a little more time. In other words, they could set up maybe six machines and six ladies could be running these machines, and he would just be supervising them. But he had the knowledge and he had to check that everything was right.

So there were specific men's jobs and specific women's jobs?

That is right. In other words, we did some of the menial part that they didn't have to do. So they did the setups and everything which took knowledge, which we would have never been able to learn in such a short time. We did, over a period of time, learn some things, but not enough to really take a machine and set it up and really work it. If there were women that were doing it — there might have been one or two that really had gone to school and gone through the training and everything — because we did take a certain amount of training at night school, but very little. But at the Harnischfeger plant we went in and they paid us more immediately, but we were working nights — it was the second shift. We worked [from 3:00 P.M. to 11:00 P.M.].

Did several women go together to apply for this?

Yes. I think there was three crane operators from Chain Belt and that we went together to apply for work. Because in numbers there's a little strength, and you need a little moral support. You're not used to looking for a job, and you didn't know what you were getting into; you were afraid at that time. We were not as bold as we are now. I guess we were not brought up in as many facets of life as kids are nowadays. We were taken into the shop and shown where we would work

Of course, at the ordnance plant everything was new, it was just a new government building. Everything was clean, everything was nice. It was a machine shop — it was not dirty, it was not smoky. Well, we walked into this building where we were supposed to work. The cranes were, oh my, about thirty feet up in the air compared to maybe about fifteen to twenty feet in the machine shop. It

WHi(X3)32696

President Franklin Roosevelt (looking through car window) and Wisconsin Governor Julius Heil (applauding) on a visit to the Allis-Chalmers plant in Milwaukee, September 19, 1942.

was a difference, and there was nothing but welding and smoke and dirt. I said, "Oh no, I don't think I choose to work in this building — no." The gentlemen who eventually was my boss said, "Rose, we need you. We really, really need you ladies. Give it a chance." I said, "Oh, Mr. Kohler, I couldn't work in all this smoke, no, please." He said, "Give it two weeks and see what you're going to say." I said, "Well . . ." Another gal looked at me and she said, "Fine, we'll try it," and I said, "Okay, we'll try it."

When we got there the fellows on the floor were so nice. If I thought I was a crane operator at Chain Belt, I was nothing at Harnischfeger, because the work was altogether different. We made car bodies and frames for excavators, earth movers, and we made government equipment, too — tractors for the government, great big tractors. We had these great big cranes and they were just huge. The frames themselves must have been a couple tons. You'd pick them up and you'd turn them and I would be just scared sick and the fellows would say, "Don't do anything unless we give you signal. You'll do it, you'll do fine." And they were really nice, and they would give me signals, and I learned how to move all this equipment and turn it over and do it and by the end of two weeks everyone was so nice that you couldn't say no, that you didn't want to work there anymore.

So the work was much more difficult at this plant?

Oh, yes. Much more difficult and you had older equipment. We did not have modern equipment that we had at the other plant. First of all, we were in the area where we did the welding and they had skylights to eliminate the smoke, so during the wintertime they opened the skylights to let the smoke go out, and the heating system did no good because it would be cold. So the fellows on the floor would take these great big huge oil drums and they'd fill it up with coke, or whatever they did, and they would make fires to heat themselves and warm themselves up and we'd get all the smoke up there. We'd open up the skylights to let the smoke go out. Even though we had heaters in the crane I would wear boots in the winter and a snowsuit right up in the crane because it was so cold and there was not a good heating system.

That has been changed over the years since. Now it's much different. The heating has been modernized and everything. But at the time, the minute you were through working you went down on the floor because you were too cold up there or you got too much smoke. You could get asphyxiated. They didn't have things like the masks and everything they do now for safety. Then we'd come down on the floor and the fellows — and I suppose maybe I shouldn't, I don't know, time has gone by and we'll let little secrets out — but the fellows, when they would be welding, they did it on a time machine. They would lay thick welds, not like a small weld. They would have real heavy, thick welds and they would lay this metal down with the rods and they would pour it, and then this little time machine would turn and turn and let them know how many hours of welding they got in so that they would be paid piecework. When they would take a break, we girls would put on the helmets, and they'd show us how to weld, and we would lay the metal down for them. We were helping, we were putting out production, right? And the guys were making more money, and we did welding. There were a lot of women welders, too, there at the time, and they did a good job. They were working in an area where it was not quite the heavy work in the area that I was in. I think the majority of women were crane operators at that time. We started out about ninety cents an hour at that time. We were getting paid more than we were at Rex Chain Belt, and I think we earned it.

How did that rate of pay compare with the welders' pay?

Oh no, the welders got more. See, they were on piecework. They were on production and we were not. We replaced all the men up there and we knew that when the boys would come back that we were out of jobs. We knew that, but we didn't care; that was okay. The nice thing is, the plant was close to home and I worked from 3:00 [P.M.] to 11:00 [P.M.]. I could walk home. We were safe to walk home. It was within walking distance and, of course, that meant that I'd go home and go to sleep, get up in the morning, and go over and pick up my daughter. I'd have her with me all day.

So, did you have the same woman taking care of your daughter when you worked second shift?

Yes. She took care of her. She was all alone. Her husband was deceased, and she had one son and he was in the service and, she was alone. So this was good for her as it was for us. I think there was about four children that she took care of on a regular basis — very, very fine woman. In fact, after my second child was born — that was after John came home and we had our second child — then when she was a little older and I went back to work again, I had [the same woman] take care of her. I don't think I would have ever worked if I didn't have this fine woman. She was really very, very nice. . . . You wonder what we did weekends? . . . We packed up my daughter and a little overnight case and we went over to Mama's. It sounds kind of childish, but you did. We went home for weekends because there was still a sister at home that was young, a lot younger than I was.

Where was this?

In Milwaukee. We just got on the bus — we walked seven blocks, I guess, to a bus line and, in fact, at the end of the bus line there was a grocery store, and the fellow in the grocery said, "Why don't you take your stroller and push your daughter in a stroller and leave it on my back porch so you don't have to carry her so far." Because, otherwise, you take a little four-year-old or three-year-old and cart her seven blocks to the bus with a suitcase. And we'd go to my mom's and, of course, that was nice. We would stay there for the weekend and have family dinner together and then you could leave the youngster with Mama and you could go to a movie maybe with your lady friends or go bowling. I remember at that time we didn't even know how to bowl, but it was something to do. We'd go get on a bowling alley and say, "What do we do?" Oh well, just roll the

*Rose Kaminski (center);
her daughter, Darlene;
and her mother, Anna
Sidoruck, on Wisconsin
Avenue in Milwaukee,
January 21, 1945.*

Courtesy Rose Kaminski, WHi(X3)48392

ball and try to hit the pins! You didn't know where to go, you didn't
know what to do, when you were without a partner.

Were you a member of the union at Harnischfeger?

Yes, we all joined the union, yes, because at that time that was up-
permost in our minds because of the protection that we got. We
knew that we would be laid off eventually, and there was no qualms
about that. There was no "We're going to fight for our rights" or
anything. We knew what we were there for; we were there to relieve
the men from their duties so that they could go into the service.
That was understandable. The union guaranteed us our prevailing
wages and I recall when I had worked there a short while — when I
say short while, I'd say maybe three months or so — and I went
over and I talked to my boss and I told him that I really thought
that for the type of work that I was doing, the area that I was working in, compared to some of the clean areas some of the other ladies
were working, that I deserved more money. And I got a $1.10 an
hour, I got a nice big raise, about a twenty-cent raise, just like that.
He agreed with me. So that was kind of nice. . . .

I worked in the one area most of the while. If we were needed in
different areas — to substitute if someone was sick and they needed
us — we had to go, but those were very minimal because the women
were pretty conscientious. They came to work regularly. They
didn't take off for things left and right. They were pretty dedicated.
I didn't get on a friendly basis with any of them as far as socializing,
because I had a daughter to come home to, and that was my biggest
thought. We did have union dances and union activities which we
could go to, but you always felt a little uncomfortable.

Why was that?

Well, you were married, your husband was in service and you were
alone and you wanted to go and you wanted to participate. Maybe
nowadays the girls wouldn't think of going to a dance without an
escort, but we did because there was no choice. You had no choice,
and in order to get out and socialize, we did it. Even though you felt
a little uncomfortable, it gave you something to do and, boy, it was
something you wanted to do besides just staying at home and being
a mother all the time.

Did you have a car during this period?

Not when my husband was in service. No, I never learned how to
drive. I always said I learned how to run an overhead crane before I

even learned how to drive. I didn't learn how to drive until, oh, many years later. That was quite exciting. . . .

When you worked in the factories, we had a cafeteria. We were allowed to eat our meals in the cafeteria. We didn't have to give any stamps up for the food that we ate there, so naturally I ate my main meal there and I would use my ration stamps for buying food for my youngster when I would come home so that I could cook for her. The nice thing is that in the cafeteria — we used to have a matron that took care of the problems of the women. We had one woman that was in charge of all the women and she would be in our restroom areas and if we had any personal problems or anything, we would deal with her. It would be a like a public relations person at this time, but it was a little bit closer and little more intimate. A very nice woman.

Was that her main job?

That was her only job. She was there for all of us. She issued us our caps and hair nets and whatever clothes that we had, too, and if they worked in certain areas and needed uniforms or anything, she issued those and took care of our locker rooms. But, anyway, she said to me, "A lot of times in the cafeteria at the end of the night they have soup left over and things left over." She said, "If you want, Rose, let me know and I will see that you can buy some soup." And I thought, oh good, because that was the hardest thing. I always worried about my daughter getting the proper food. So she said, "Bring a jar to work from home, and we'll fill it up and we'll charge you for it, and you can take it home." So, I did that. I would bring home soup for my daughter and, of course, in that quart jar that would be enough for myself and her. We'd have a nice meal out of it, and then you'd be saving stamps, too, so, you would have stamps for other food. And you never felt that you were depriving anybody because this would be extra, over and above, that they wouldn't use. It would be wasted otherwise, and it was good. So, I did that. That was very nice and it saved me a lot of time in cooking, too, and it helped.

Did you pool stamps when you went to your mother's on the weekend?

Oh, yes we did. I had two other sisters, too, and when they came over — we all shared together — we would put stamps together and get a nice roast. . . . Mother would go shopping for nylons for the girls because there was four girls in the family. She would be able to stand in the lines for maybe an hour, two hours, bless her

Courtesy Rose Kaminski. WHi(X3)48394

Women workers at Harnischfeger Corporation having a Christmas party in the locker room, ca. 1944. Rose Kaminski is the first seated woman on the left.

heart, just to get nylons for the ladies, the girls, and we would get our nylons.

What was shopping like for you, especially as a working mother whose husband was away?

First of all, about the biggest shopping I did was either grocery shopping, and that was about three–four blocks away from home, and our butcher was one we knew personally because we had shopped there for so many years. It's not like hopping in a car and going to the malls and buying whatever you want, or the great big supermarkets. There was the small grocery store and there was a butcher and a drugstore on the corner, so you know all those people over the years, personally, and your butcher would know his old customers and not people that just came because they were trying to get something special from him. He would kind of cater to his regular customers because he knew who was working in the war plants, and the grocery men [knew], too. So that part of it was not too bad.

You didn't always get what you wanted. You had to take what they had on hand. Even at that time the government used to issue recipe books, or "101 Different Ways to Fix Hamburger." Boy, we learned how to fix hamburger all the different ways. In fact, I just recently gave my cookbook away to a young lady who collects recipe books and she couldn't get over all the recipes that were in there.

Did you eat differently during the war?

Not really, because we were poor. We were poor before and we had to stretch that dollar before, and we made a go of it and I don't see that we ate less than we did before. It was frugal and, of course, it was nice eating in the cafeteria because there we got more than we would have probably had at home. When we were at weekends at my mother's, my mother was a terrific cook. When we were kids, and we were on the county [assistance], my dad worked seasonal work at the Nash Kelvinator plant, where they would work nine months out of the year and three months there was no work because they had change of models and then they closed the plant down. So then my mother had to get assistance sometimes for us when Dad wasn't working, because there was five kids at home. So, whatever she got she learned how to cook well with what she had, and she was terrific. I don't know to this day how she did it. I don't think I could have. She could make anything from nothing. We always ate good. We *always* ate good. She would bake with whatever she had and she would cook with whatever she had and it was good.

Was it important to your family that you marry a Polish boy? Did you live in a predominantly Polish neighborhood?

There were quite a few people in the neighborhood that were Polish. I'm going to backtrack way to when I was a youngster. I was four years old when my dad died and my mother was left with four children. . . . When my dad was living, we lived in a predominantly Jewish neighborhood. My dad was a cobbler, a shoemaker. There was four of us, and, like I said, we were poor. We lived in a one-room house in the back of the shoe repair shop. . . . The people in the neighborhood would say, "How do you do this? How do you keep your children so nice and clean, how do you keep them dressed so nice?" [My mother] said, "You have to work," and she did. The people on the corner had a grocery store, and they were Jewish, and, of course, the Jews were really picked on. They were called — I'm not going to mention names, but they were called all different names. Then, my mother used to say, "You don't do that, you don't

Rose Kaminski, 1945.

Courtesy Rose Kaminski: WHi(X3)48393

do that. These people are good to us, they are friendly to us. You judge people by what they are, not by what nationality or religion or anything." So, we got along fine. In fact, when there was a Jewish grandmother and grandfather in the neighborhood and they used to have a little gazebo in the back yard and they used to do their ceremonies in the back yard, [and] we were invited to them. They really let us come in and see what they were doing, and it was nice. They really were good to us, and we learned a lot from them, and I think they learned from us. They learned that my mother did give the kids a little sausage once in a while. They're not supposed to have it, but she just thought it was just terrible that somebody couldn't eat the little hot dogs. That was the kind of the person she was.

Well, then Dad died, and we moved out and we went on this mother's pension, and Mother decided she was going to go to work. We lived in an Italian neighborhood, and that was at the time the Italians were being picked on. It just seemed that if you were going from one neighborhood to another neighborhood people were being ostracized, and for no reason at all. People were calling them wops, and my mother said, "I don't ever want to hear you call those people that. Those are good people. You judge people by who they are." She went into a hosiery company and worked, and the fellows that were in the plant used to give her extra piecework so she could make more money for her four children. And she said, "Those men are good and the people are good." And the people above us were Italian, and "You don't call them names." It was a good, good background to be brought up in. She was very understanding. So then my mother remarried, and my dad, who was a bachelor, married a woman with four orphans and he was good to us. He was good to us until the day that he passed away — bless his heart.

What would you say was the ethnic background of most of the people who worked at Harnischfeger?

Quite a few German. The company officials were very much so, German. They came from Germany. But the beautiful part of working there is I have seen where handicapped people were hired to work in that plant, and black people were hired at a time when minorities were not hired and handicaps were not hired. I remember one particular case where there was a man whose one arm was debilitated that it was hard for him to climb a ladder and get into a crane, and he was hired because the grandfather, Mr. Harnischfeger, had a handicap himself, and they never discriminated against the handicapped, which I thought was wonderful.

And black people — that was not a time when a lot of black people were hired, but I remember there were black people that were hired. I also remember when we worked at the supercharger plant when one of the girls had a friend who was black — a very close friend — and everybody was just shocked. They thought she was just — ahh! She was daring that she would even go in to the black neighborhood and associate with the blacks. It was the exposure we never had. It isn't that I would be afraid to associate with anyone of that color. That never bothered me. In fact, I have had black friends over the years, but at that time it was kind of shocking. It was daring, it was different, and everybody talked about her. I thought, "Well, she has a right to choose her own friends." . . .

[After the war ended,] by the time things settled down and the fellows were released, I would say it was a good six months or more before they were released and they were allowed to come home. By that time, one by one, the servicemen were coming back to work and they always got priority and they would replace us one by one. Finally, the fellow that I replaced came, and I remember him coming back and I was laid off.

How did you feel about that?

It didn't bother me, because you knew it was there. It wouldn't be like you're working and all of a sudden someone came up to you and said that you were terminated within a week or two weeks, and it would be something that you didn't anticipate. We knew it. I think we even kind of looked forward to it.

In what way?

Well, that you could get back to normal living. What was normal living? I don't know what normal living was, because we were so average. We just got back into the old routine. My husband came home, he went back to his old job, and it was not what he wanted, and he got a different job. The money was a little better and we moved and in the process of moving, and upgrading our living conditions, I just happened to call my former boss and asked him if they were hiring women, because there were a lot of men that did not come back.

How long was that? You were off the job for how long?

Oh, I would say at least a year. Oh, longer than that, because in the meantime my youngest daughter was born, and I think she must have been, oh, about three years after that, because she was about three years old when I went back to work. I just called on the spur of the moment to ask my old boss if there were any openings for women anymore. I thought, "Gee, it would be nice to be able to work just enough to pay for moving expenses and buying some more new furniture for a larger flat." He said, "Well, there's a job opening for about six weeks. One of the fellows broke his leg and we would like to have somebody replace him for six weeks." And I said, "That would be perfect. Six weeks of money would help a lot at this time." I said, "Well, can I call you back? First I have to find out who's going to take care of my children for me," because I had two girls at that time. And I asked this grandma across the street if she would, and she said sure she would. So I called back and I said, "Yes, I can do it for six weeks." Well, that six weeks extended until I retired here about eleven years ago, and I have thirty-one years with the company, so that's quite an extension, isn't it?

*   *   *   *   *

Evelyn Gotzion

Born in Waunakee, near Madison, in 1913, Evelyn (Bailey) Gotzion grew up in Madison and married Steven Gotzion in 1931. The couple had three children, born in 1932, 1933, and 1940. In 1935, Gotzion began work at Rayovac, a manufacturer of batteries and lighting products, and remained there for the next forty-three years, actively participating in union activities. She was widowed in 1975 and continues to reside in Madison.

How did you arrange for child care during the war?

I had a daughter that was about eight and the other boy was probably six and then the little guy, when the war first started out. So my sister was there until he got older and then she went to work at Oscar Mayer's because there they had to make all the meats to send over to the war, so she had no problem getting a job, and they made good money. Then she had another girlfriend that came in and when I started sending my boy to nursery school and didn't have to have a full-time housekeeper anymore, then this girlfriend came and the two of them had me buy a studio couch and put in my dining room so they could sleep down there. Then my father-in-law moved home with me because my sister-in-law and brother-in-law, because of his job, got transferred to Minneapolis. So Grandpa didn't have no place to stay, and he worked at the Gisholt Machine Company, [which] was also war work. So he lived at my house. Well, then we ended up building a room on our house because we didn't have enough room. At one time I had nine people at my house, and it was quite an ordeal.

We'd sit by the kitchen table having our dinner at night, and we'd decide what are we going to have tomorrow night, and it was something I could start for my husband to put in the oven for us. We would like hot dishes or something like that or get a roast ready. The boys would tell me what they'd like and Grandpa and them and the girls what they should have. And they all worked. Everybody worked, everybody had to do something; yes, everybody did something. And on Saturdays, or the days we were home, it was the washing. And if I wasn't there and the girls had some time off, they'd do and they'd pitch in and help. So everybody helped everybody. Even my mother used to come over once in a while and she'd bake for us on Saturday morning or Friday morning so we'd have some home-baked goods because by the time we'd get home we were tired. To just do our everyday work was a lot, keeping up a home and a family.

How long was your average workday?

Well, we used to work eight hours, and then it got to be nine hours and then ten hours. Many times we worked ten hours a day and eleven hours a day. If they had some order to get out, they'd ask everybody if they'd stay and help so they could get it out. And we'd work, like say, six in the morning, sometimes we'd start at seven. . . . Nobody ever took off work hardly because you didn't dare. They just needed you so bad and you felt like you had to do your share too. . . .

And when we'd go to the store, I had only a half an hour for my lunch lot of days but I'd take my sandwich and eat it as I went up and down the aisle and I would start the grocery shopping and my husband would meet me. And the girl up there, she knew things — about a big order in there every week — and if there were certain things rationed and she'd gotten them during the week, she was kind enough to always save me some so I'd have some, because she figured that people that shopped there all the time should have, and then I worked and couldn't come in there other ways. Then [my husband would] take the groceries home and put them away for me. [He would do] everything that he could.

What did you do at Rayovac?

I had all kinds of jobs. Then we had one line, a big line, where when you'd work ten hours and you'd stand in one spot or sit in one spot. It got terrible, all day long. So I suggested to my foreman, the general foreman, that we take turns of learning everybody's job and switching every half hour. Well, they didn't like it, but we were on the side, every once in a while, learning each other's job and learning how to do it, so eventually most all of us got so we could do all the jobs, [of] which there was probably fifteen or twenty on the line. We could do every job so we could go up and down the line and rotate. And then they found out that that was a really pretty good thing to do because it made the people happier, and they could take each other's place when they went to the bathroom. There wasn't that many extra people to get around there if you had to go into the nurse or something to take your place. And the foremen were so busy, they couldn't come. And then we had government inspectors that walked around there and checked everything we did.

So it worked out real great, but we had a lot of problems trying to consent to letting them do it. I know this one day, this one lady and I had changed jobs and my boss said, "What are you doing

WHi(X3)46247

A woman worker demonstrates pressing operations at the Badger Ordnance Works near Baraboo.

down in this position?" I said, "I am doing her job, and she's doing mine." I said, "If you don't think I can do it right, the government inspector was just here, Ed was just here, he said I'm doing fine." My inspector was here now. I said, 'Why don't you stand here, too, and then when you get done with me, you go up and see her."

Did the union help convince management to allow you to switch jobs?

No, no. This was just my idea because we got so tired of standing in one spot. But then one day I was the steward, and they wouldn't listen to me. They cut our rates, and so I shut off the line and the boss came up and he said, "What are you doing?" I said, "Well, I have asked everybody that I know why we have gotten a cut in pay and why we're doing exactly the same amount of work as we did. The only thing you did was change your box down there and you open it from another end. That's all I can see that's different. I went up and down the line, I've talked to everybody. There's nothing different. How can you change our job?" [He said,] "Well, you turn that line on, or I'm going to send you into the office." I said, "I wish you'd send me into the office." "Well," he said, "You turn the line on and I'll get you somebody down here to talk to." So the rate setter came down and I said, "Would you please explain it and write it out on a piece of paper, because all these people on this line are real interested to know what's going on." He said, "No, I have a right to set the rate the way I want to and I see how it's done." I think [that] when we all could do each other's job and they found it out efficiently, they maybe thought it was too easy for us or something.

So, anyhow, we wrote up a big grievance and they all signed it and then I called the president of the union and then we had a meeting and then we had the other stewards in on it. Then we called our Milwaukee office and they sent a man in, and they said they thought we had a good grievance, and so then we had a meeting with the management and at that point the president decided that I should be added to the bargaining committee so that I would go in and argue our case, because I could do it better than any of the rest of them could because I knew what it was. So I went along in to the management with the union.

First of all, they wanted to know what I was doing there. I was not a union executive. [I was no] more than a steward, and when had we changed our policy, and then they went on to tell them what had happened. We argued it, [and] then they brought in another guy from someplace else, the company did, and then we did. We finally got it straightened out, and we got our back pay, too. From then on I was on the bargaining committee all the years that I worked at Rayovac. I was never voted off the committee because if I thought there was something right I wasn't afraid to argue for it and fight for it. I didn't care whose toes I stepped on, really. If it was right, it was right. Well, management wasn't very kind to me for a while. But when there was something to do in the plant like solicit for United Givers and all of that, they always asked me to do it. I guess I didn't hurt myself too much. At least I felt better because I knew it was right and we had two or three real older ladies, lot older than me, working on that line and they worked hard and I knew they were dragging when night come, they were so tired out, and I thought, "Why should they work for less money? The government is paying the company all this money and they're getting it all. Why aren't we getting some of it? We should have something, too."

2

Young, Single, and Working

EVEN before America's entry into World War II, most single women sought and found paid employment, although in most cases they left their jobs when they married. Thus, the participation of single women in the labor force represented a continuation of prewar practices. Because social opportunities involving men were severely limited during the war, co-workers often provided these women with a social network through both company-sponsored and informal recreational events. Spending so much time with a group of people inevitably led to involvements that extended past the office door, as co-workers shared each others' worries and celebrations.

Dating itself took on different aspects as well. First, because few young, single men remained — most had joined the military — dating opportunities became much more scarce. Many young women actively participated in social activities sponsored by the USO (United Service Organizations), which established recreational clubs for those in the service. Women who attended USO dances not only met young men but also felt that they were contributing to the war effort. Second, marriage rates increased, in part because the improved economy allowed marriages that had been delayed because of the depression and in part because marriages often took place much more quickly than they would have under different circumstances: the imminent departure of young men for war lent a sense of urgency not present in other times. These marriages (and those of couples who put off their weddings until the war's end) set the stage for the postwar baby boom. Finally, the common practice of casually dating visiting servicemen sometimes led to problems — these men were strangers, and there was really no way to verify their backgrounds and good intentions. In the vast majority of cases, however, these excursions resulted only in afternoons or evenings of fun for the men stationed far away from home and for the women who entertained them.

Luida Sanders, who worked as a teacher in small towns in northern Wisconsin, and Emily Koplin and Dorothy Zmuda, who worked in offices in Milwaukee, illustrate what it was like to be young, single, and working during the war. They vividly depict the sense of freedom and independence felt by young women at that time as well as the various aspects of their work and social lives.

Luida Sanders

Born in Rhinelander in 1917, Luida Sanders grew up in a series of towns in northern Wisconsin, including Lake Tomahawk, Wittenberg, West De Pere, and Styles Junction. After graduating from high school in 1934, Sanders worked for part of one year in Racine and for two years at the courthouse in Shawano to save enough money to continue her education. She received a two-year rural teaching certificate from Stevens Point State Teachers College in 1939 and then spent four years as a rural schoolteacher, in Brown and Shawano counties. In 1943, as soon as she could get out of her teaching contract, she joined the Women's Auxiliary Army Corps (WAAC), which later became the Women's Army Corps (WAC), rising to the rank of technical sergeant. She served as a recruitment officer, secretary, and hospital worker and was stationed in Massachusetts, Alabama, and Georgia. After her discharge from the service in 1946, Sanders used the GI Bill to obtain a bachelor's degree in education from the University of Wisconsin. She later obtained a master's degree in public administration from the UW and a master's degree in public health from the University of California at Berkeley. Since the war, she has pursued a career in public health in Wisconsin, and she currently resides in Oshkosh.

In 1937 I went to Stevens Point Teachers College and took the two-year rural [teaching] course. It seemed to be the only option that I had. Never considered any other work. I knew I didn't want to sit typing the rest of my life. The second year I borrowed two hundred dollars from my aunt and I got a part-time job. I finished the year with what I had saved, and then my two years. Then I got a teaching contract for eighty-nine dollars a month.

The first school was in the town of Poland, out from Green Bay. That was just an interesting school. In 1939 there were a lot of people from "the old country" and one of the first things the board did after I got there was buy a battery radio so I could turn it on and get the news on what was happening over in the old country so the kids could bring it home — information — because a lot of them didn't have radios. Most of the kids talked Polish so out in the playground they'd be talking away and I'd just listen — of course, I didn't talk a word of Polish. But it was a nice school. I enjoyed my two years

*Luida Sanders (standing) with her class at the Gray Hill School in
Poland, Brown County, fall, 1939.*

there. And then after the second year my father died, and I needed
to be home with Mother, so I could live at home. I then got the
school out near Wittenberg and taught at Hidden Valley School for
two years before going into service. I liked rural teaching — a lot of
independence, very challenging.

What kind of guidance did you have?

There was a county supervisor who came around about twice a year
and stayed for maybe two or three hours, something like that.
That's about it. The year before my dad died I went to summer
school, but after that I had to work because Mother didn't have any
income. There was nothing once he died. His pension ended, and
she wasn't able to work. I thought she was terribly old. She was
thirty-nine when I was born, so by the time I was in my twenties she
was up in her sixties and not too well. So I was back at Wittenberg.

What range of ages and grades did you teach?

First grade through eighth — both of them were all eight grades.
. . . The schools in the area of Wittenberg in Shawano County
had — you wouldn't call it a league, but we had softball and so we

played all spring. We had games at different schools on Friday afternoon. The parents would take the team around. I'm afraid I wasn't much of a coach, because we never won very much, except that we had a very good pitcher. One of our boys was so good at pitching that he pitched on the men's team in the summer. . . . He was the only reason we ever won a game. He could also bat.

Was this a coed team?

No, just boys. Oh no, wait. No, it was coed; they were coed, that's right, because one of these girls was very good at running particularly. If she could get on base she would really make it all around.

You taught for about a year and a half after the war began. How was that different than the first three years that you taught?

Oh, I don't remember that it was terribly different. We usually had that little discussion of current events at [the] opening [of class]. You know, what did you read in the paper, that sort of thing. [We] would talk about the war. Then, visiting with the children at recess and lunch, we'd ask about their relatives who were in service, what they'd heard about so and so, if [he] finished training and was shipping out and that sort of thing. But other than that I don't think the actual classes changed at all.

Was everyone in your class pretty much touched by the war?

I think the families seemed to have — yeah, they seemed to be. In order to teach at Hidden Valley School I had to have a car, so I bought a '37 Chevy in Green Bay. I had learned to drive a Model T when I was in high school because we were four miles out and the only way we could get there was to drive, so I drove the Model T. My brother would get out and crank it. So I knew how to steer at least. So then when I bought the '37 Chevy in order to teach at Hidden Valley School, the salesman took me out on the road and said, "Well, just make sure that you can handle the car all right." Oh, maybe two hours or so driving around. That's all the driver education I had, and then I just mailed in my quarter and got my license. That was all there was to it. I remember driving from Green Bay to Wittenberg. The first year or so I drove where I looked, I steered where I looked. So if I looked off the side, I steered off to the side. My cousin had ridden up with me that first time, and I remember her saying, "Oh, the moon is coming up, but don't look."

Was there a problem with the younger kids who might have been more frightened by the war?

I don't recall there was any conscious effort to deal with that. I would visit with the kids as I always did at recess. Eat lunch with them at noon and they'd come early or some stayed late after school and talk and I always asked them about, you know, have you heard from your brother or uncle or father or whatever. I think it was just a sharing; it wasn't a conscious effort to deal with their psychology.

*   *   *   *   *

Emily Koplin

Born in Milwaukee in 1926, Emily Koplin grew up in an ethnically diverse neighborhood on Milwaukee's south side. Koplin's father was of German descent; her mother was of French descent and grew up in Canada. Koplin has worked in the office at the Allen-Bradley Company since graduating from high school in 1943, and at age sixty-seven she continues to postpone retirement.

What were some of the first changes that you can recall occurring in your life as a result of the war?

The rationing. I think the part that hurt us the most was the gas rationing and the tightness of food — meat. I remember my mother going to grocery stores and coming home with just a small package of whatever. There was no variety, [and] whatever they had, she bought.

What was dating like during the war?

The girls that I knew all had boyfriends who were in the service and we didn't date because we were "tagged." I was going out with a fellow that was in the air force and I had his wings and he also sent me his lieutenant wings. . . . I spent a lot of time with the girls that I worked with [at Allen-Bradley] who had boyfriends or husbands overseas. There wasn't much dating going on. Most of the girls had engagement rings and we were all busy writing letters and corresponding, so the dating was mostly girls with girls. I don't know about the others, but that's the crowd that I went with. We waited for our men to come home. We didn't do any dating — those were the years where we would go to dances and girls would dance with girls. We had good times; we had a lot of fun. We were very, very close because we were all waiting for [our men] to come back home. We had a lot in common and were very close.

Emily Koplin, Milwaukee, 1944.

Courtesy Emily Koplin. WHi(X3)48503

What sorts of things would you do when you would go out with your girlfriends?

We went to a lot of movies. . . . We did a lot of dancing, and we spent a lot of time — we used to spend days down at the parks and down at the lakefront posing for pictures. It sounds so silly now, but we used to spend days posing for pictures and sunbathing so that it would look good in the pictures.

Even though there was rationing, we used to go out a lot. I remember never going home after work. We used to always go someplace and eat and then the girls would get together at somebody's house. We played ping-pong, we played cards, we bowled, we did a lot of just really nothing. We kept busy. We used to have ping-pong tournaments to see who the champion was, and we really worked at it. We spent whole nights beating each other to see who the winner was. We just enjoyed ourselves completely. We used to go to baseball games. And, of course, once I joined Allen-Bradley, Allen-Bradley held baseball games. The company belonged to an industrial league. We also had basketball games right here in the shop. We used to go up to the gym in evenings and I was part of the Allen-

Bradley Dramatic Club. We used to put on shows here and we'd
have to rehearse nights. So, we kept busy, very busy.

*Do you think there was a special sense of camaraderie among women
during the war?*

Yes, very definitely.

*What did that mean to you in terms of creating friendships among
women?*

My family — I had a mother and a father and a brother. When I
started working here at Allen-Bradley, and of course those were the
war years, all the girls — we were very, very close. It was like we
were all sisters. There was a closeness that you don't have today. A
lot of the girls that were working here were from out of town, didn't
have families in Milwaukee. . . . We were much closer than the
women are today, much closer. And we all cried on each other's
shoulders and we knew everything about everybody. We knew
when they got letters from their boyfriends, we knew when they
didn't feel good, we knew when they were going home to, let's say,
Pulaski, Wisconsin. We knew just exactly where we all were almost
on an hourly basis. It was a very close knit — the women were stuck
together much more than today. . . .

It was very important to have somebody to lean on, to have
somebody to just talk to. Here's a situation where even though I
was at home with my mother and my father, I couldn't relate to
them like I related to these other gals because we all had the same
feelings about what was happening. And the mothers and the fathers, they were worried about their sons being overseas, not necessarily the daughter that was left back home. They were concentrat-
ing on bringing their boys back home. So I think that that's one of
the reasons why the girls — that we did become as friendly as we
did with one another.

Was the war the crucial element in bringing women together?

Yes, I believe so. Because we all had so much in common and
leaned on one another. I don't think that would have happened if
the girls would have been married to these gentlemen and would
have started their families. Then they would have had their separate
lives and gone [their separate ways], because that's what happened
when the war ended. That's what happened with the war. As these
men came home and the girls married and they started having their
families then all of a sudden those of us who weren't married or

A 1943 U.S. Army poster saluting female officeworkers' contributions to the war effort.

SECRETARIES OF WAR

didn't get married, then you're not part of that pattern anymore. They would go their way and you would go your way. The ending of the war made everybody go in "their own directions."

What were your social relationships with co-workers like?

We worked Monday through Friday, we worked a half a day on Saturday, and then on Sundays we would be a part of this USO activity and spend the whole days at the USO centers sponsored by Allen-Bradley. So we really spent almost a whole week [together], not only on our job, but as part of the Allen-Bradley entertainment group. So we spent a lot of time together. There was very little time that we spent away from one another, and I think that's where the closeness came in. We were always together. I think the only time that anybody did anything separate was on Saturday night. That sounds weird, but I think even then we were at somebody's house, that we were doing something with one another. I think we spent the better part of our lives with one another. But there wasn't that much [to do], there were limitations. You couldn't, like today, you couldn't get in a car and go anywhere. You couldn't spend any time on the road because of gas rationing. You couldn't do much traveling, so you had to find your activity right around the home front or the office front, whatever you want to call it.

Were all your workplace social relations with women? Were there men as well?

There were men, there were still men that were here. It wasn't strictly a "woman company." There were men here, but social-wise the men that were here during those years were men that were married and had families but for one reason or another were not in the service. Except for being at company functions, where the men were, they were usually with their wives or their families.

Did your family do any gardening during the war?

No, we didn't, we never did, except for an occasional tomato bush or something. . . . My father worked for a commission company and across the street from the commission row they had a farmers' market, and my dad used to bring bushels of fresh fruit and vegetables from the farmers' market. They would sell for like a dollar, and we would eat tomatoes in everything possible for weeks. We were lucky, we had this farmers' market factor. My dad would get whatever the farmers would bring in and my mother was good at arranging meals around whatever was available. I can't say that we ever suffered food-wise, but it was different than the eating styles of today.

Did you encounter any anti-German or anti-Italian feeling during this time?

Oh, yes. The Germans lived on the north side, the Polish people lived on the south side, the Italians lived on the east side. We had a Third Ward, and everybody who was Italian lived in the Third Ward. You have to appreciate, my father was German, my mother was French, and when my mother bought our house on the south side, my father's people told my dad that he could come back and stay at home any time he wanted to. His family would never come across the viaduct to visit us because we were on the south side. People didn't do it. You stayed within your group, you stayed within your nationality. If you were German, you married German. If you were Polish, you married Polish, and if you were Italian, you married Italian.

My mother was the opposite. She grabbed my dad and she decided she was going to pull him out of all of that. . . . My mother was never accepted by my dad's family, never. You have to appreciate, my mother was born in New Orleans, Louisiana; my mother's [of] French descent. She was raised in Canada, went to school in Canada, and when she married my dad, my dad's family told him that my mother should go back where she came from. . . . Every Sunday afternoon my dad's family all met at Grandma Koplin's home; that was a ritual. [The children] would go to Borchert Field, which was just west of where they lived. The daughters and the son-in-laws would meet at Grandma and Grandpa Koplin's. And my mother went every Sunday afternoon, and they talked nothing but German, and my mother sat there every afternoon on a Sunday out of respect for my dad. They never let her in. It was sad. There were only two of my dad's sisters that would come on the south side and visit us. That was something you just didn't do. It was pathetic, it really, truly was. But we survived, we survived.

Did the people on the south side make you feel like interlopers?

Not at all, not at all. The family living north of us were Italians and here we were, they were Italians and here we were German and French. I can't remember what nationality the Baumans were just south of us. I think they were a German family, and there was never any problem on our side. Now the strange part of it is, the south side was Polish and yet in our neighborhood we never had any Polish people. Not at the beginning, not at the start. We were all different and there was never any problem. The Italian family that we had living next door to us drank nothing but wines. Their daughter, Audrey, never drank water at home. She would come over to our house to get a glass of water, because her people never served water at home. . . . . We're still friends and that goes back from the thirties. That's a long way. [My brother and I] were four and five years old at the time and my mother established the nicest relationship with her mother and dad and I still see Audrey about once or twice a year when she's in Milwaukee. There's some good things to be said. What happened on the south side wasn't like what happened on the north side. It was an entirely different feeling. If you were German you married German and you stayed German. That's what it amounted to. They would talk only in German — they never let my mother in. It was pathetic.

Was there any overt anti-German feeling here because of the war?

I can't comment on that because that was something that we never discussed at our house because, again, of our German and French ties and the trouble that we had with the German side of the family.

We never went into the Adolf Hitler story. I think it was because we never wanted to get, family-wise, involved with any of that. We never discussed Mussolini, we never discussed Adolf Hitler. We knew what he did, we knew what he stood for, we knew what was happening, but those discussions we avoided at our house. Because my mother had some very, very bad feelings about the German people in general, so we just avoided that completely.

Were those bad feelings exacerbated by your father's family?

Oh yes, yes. That's what it amounted to, so we just avoided that completely. I can remember talking about it with friends and, you know, talking about Adolf Hitler and what he was trying to accomplish and my mother used to get very, very upset about this super-race theory of his, and that bothered her something terrible. I remember her talking to us kids about that, about what he was trying to accomplish by mating these people so that he would have this super race. But we never talked about that with my dad. My dad was never part of that. My mother kept that separate; she kept that away from him so that there wouldn't be any either trouble or hard feelings so then my dad couldn't go back to his family and say, "Guess what they were talking about today." We avoided that as best as we possibly could. And I think that was a smart move — very, very smart. So whatever discussions we had about the German activity, that was between us kids or what we read in the paper and our friends and that type of a thing.

What kind of volunteer organizations were you involved in?

The USO — I was given permission by my family and I didn't do anything that my family didn't approve of, and my mother and father didn't want me getting terribly involved with a lot of different of these activities because I don't think that they completely understood what they were, even this USO business. When I told my mother that I was going downtown to dance with sailors she almost had a nervous breakdown because nice girls just didn't do that kind of thing. You have to appreciate that was the thinking back then and being seventeen years old I was part of the USO because it was sponsored here by Allen-Bradley; this is where I worked, and my mother considered that safe.

What were the USO functions like?

Well, through Allen-Bradley, of course, we were told that we had to be — I can't remember if it was here at Allen-Bradley or if it had to be downtown — but we were told where we had to be at a certain time and we would meet the North Shore train down at the depot. And when these servicemen came in, they came in knowing that they were going to be entertained by us — it was all set up ahead of time. There were just so many that were involved — there were so many girls and so many men and we spent the days with these gentlemen.

We used to pick them up from the stations. We used to take them to these different halls. Some of them were veterans' posts. We would have lunches and some of these veterans' posts were near South Shore Park and we would walk over to the lake. These were all gentlemen that were from other than Wisconsin, and we would show them whatever part of town we were in. We did a lot of walking. We would walk to the lakefront or we would walk downtown and show them the different facilities. And then somewhere along the line the dance would start and then we'd have to take them back to the North Shore Depot at a certain time, so we would pick them up and we would take them back to the depot.

We would spend a day with them or an afternoon and early evening. . . . We spent a lot of time walking, just showing them the different sights of Milwaukee, Wisconsin. They used to love coming to Milwaukee. . . . They used to love going down to Lake Michigan. We used to sit on the park benches and watch the water, okay, doing nothing but talking and looking around, and then they'd say, "Now, I'm from Philadelphia, Pennsylvania, and we don't have this type of thing where I come from, and is this beautiful." We'd spend time and then, of course, there would be other couples that would come up to us, and you'd start talking to them and [say], "Well, now, where are you from?" We just had a very enjoyable time just being friends. They wanted to see Milwaukee and whatever area we were in, we'd show them Milwaukee.

*   *   *   *   *

Dorothy Zmuda

Born in Stevens Point in 1923, Dorothy (Roshak) Zmuda moved to Milwaukee in 1942, where she worked at Allis-Chalmers as an advertising layout artist. She returned to Stevens Point in 1945 and married George Zmuda the following year. She worked as a secretary and as a clerk until the birth of the first of their five children, in 1948. Since that time, she has been a homemaker and artist. The Zmudas still reside in Stevens Point.

Courtesy Dorothy Zmuda. WHi(X3)48547.
The April Fool's Dance at the Royal Order of Funmakers
(ROOF), Milwaukee, 1944.

Did many women think that they needed to scramble for boyfriends
because there was a shortage of men?

I don't know if that's what they felt, but they were coming to work
all the time with engagement rings. . . . And then there were USO
parties and then, of course, if you went downtown in Milwaukee
there were men everywhere. You went out on Wisconsin Avenue, it
was just jammed with sailors, soldiers, marines — everything. I
don't know about during the week because I very seldom went during the week, but weekends it was bedlam out there. You could pick
up a man anywhere, any hall, anything; it was just jammed with
people. But the girls would come to the office, they were always
talking about their boyfriends. In fact, they thought I was just an
old maid because I didn't have a ring and I didn't have a steady
boyfriend. I never had a steady boyfriend so they would sort of
chide me about that. . . . Some of them would say, "Gee, Dorothy, you're the only one that doesn't have a boyfriend." I said, "I
don't want a boyfriend. I know what a boyfriend means." I said, "I
have one married brother and two married sisters, and I brought up
a couple of kids already. I changed plenty of diapers. I don't want

Dorothy Zmuda at work in the advertising department at Allis-Chalmers, Milwaukee, December 15, 1944.

Courtesy Dorothy Zmuda. WHi(X3)48500

that. Boyfriends mean babies." That's what I would tell them, "I don't want that."

So, but, yeah, they were always talking about engagement rings and some would have an engagement ring for a little while and then they'd come back and they'd have another engagement ring. In fact, I was offered an engagement ring. I forgot all about it all this time; God, I forgot all about it. Yeah, there was a young engineer that used to come down to see me. There were a lot of men [who] came to the advertising department but one day he asked me for a date. I think I went out with him twice, maybe three times, and then they would leave. You know, when they were graduated, they would leave. So he was leaving pretty soon.

To go into the service?

To go in the service, evidently, yeah. He was kind of a nice young man, but I didn't know anything about him. He was really shy. I think I was the first girl he ever probably went with, I don't know. He was rather shy, but he was just a friend. So one day, we went to the movies and out to dinner and he came and all of a sudden he pulls out a ring and says, "I'm going to be leaving pretty soon." He says, "Will you take my engagement ring?" Well, I was surprised, really. I said, "I don't even know you, and I have to say no. I don't want it." I said, "We're too young, and I don't know your family. You don't know anything about me, and I don't know anything about you," and so I have to say no to him. I never told the other girls because they would have been, you know. I just said, "No, I'm sorry."

How do you think they would have reacted?

They would have been shocked that I got a ring because I didn't have a boyfriend. Well, I went out. I didn't stay home all the time. I went to dances and things and I had dates, but I just didn't have a steady boyfriend. So I just told him no. But it was sad in a way, because I don't think he really loved me — he just wanted to have a girl. This was a lot of the thing about it. They would give a girl a ring because they wanted to leave and [be] thinking, "Well, I've got this girl to come home to." And so that's what I told him, I says, "You're just doing this because you want to be sure," and I says, "You'll find another girl. You hardly know me." So anyway, a couple of weeks later he came to me and he said, "So and so took my ring." He says, "I gave it to some other girl." And I knew her by sight, I didn't know her otherwise, and I said, "Well, gee, I'm really happy for you, and I hope you have a happy marriage," and like this and that. But I felt real sad for him that he felt that he had to give a ring to someone before he left.

But that was another sign of the times, I think. They just had to be engaged to somebody before they left, or the girl had to be engaged before they left, or some of them got married before they went and then these marriages broke up or they met someone else. That's where the "Dear Johns" came in — you know, Dear John letters. But, no, I just said no, and I don't think I told anybody about it. I just didn't say anything because I felt they would razz him and he'd have a tough time and he had a tough enough time being turned down. But I did turn him down. . . .

The other reason I didn't take a ring was because of the thing with the "Dear Jane" letter. One of the girls was engaged when I got to Allis-Chalmers. She was engaged to a young man that she had known for several years, probably from college, and she was a very nice lady and they were planning this wedding. Now these girls — I came from this small town and had nothing. I was a little Polish girl from across the slough, and in Stevens Point if you came from across the slough, yuck! But anyway here I am with these people, and many of them were very wealthy, lived on the east side, and this girl was very nice and she was planning her wedding, and of course they included me in everything immediately. They were very nice. The people there were just wonderful. They didn't care what I looked like, what I wore, who I was — I was in. I worked there and I was in.

Anyway, they were planning her wedding, so I learned all about place settings, silver, china. This was all new to me. I knew about a hope chest, but that was all. And we had showers. Oh, we bought her place settings that she chose, and her china and everything. Oh, we were so excited, this big wedding is coming up. And then Mary, she had gone to see him and she came home and they were planning the wedding and a little while, I don't know how long, just before the wedding she got the letter. "Sorry, I was with a girl in California, and she's pregnant, and I feel that I have to marry her. She's carrying my baby." Well, I tell you, that was like the end of the world for all of us — all of us, I mean. We just were shattered, everybody — the men, the women, everybody in that office was just shattered, so that I wasn't going to have any of that either. I didn't want that either. So that was why I didn't get connected to anybody. I'd go out and that was it. If they got a little romantic, I was done with that. I was too young, I was too young, and I was. So that's how that went.

Then there was another case of another gal that became engaged to a young man and he was, oh, very tall and handsome, and he came out [to the advertising department] in his uniform. He was a trainee up there at Allis-Chalmers, and he come out in his uniform. He was so handsome and she fell in love with him and he fell in love with her and they got engaged and he was leaving, too. He went out to California and she got this wonderful, gorgeous diamond ring that she helped him choose — whew, it was a monster. They were madly in love. Well, anyway, she went out to see him and either on the way to California or on the way back by train — you didn't take airplanes then — she met another sailor. He was just a plain sailor, and she talked to him and then she said, "Oh yeah, I'll write to you." Well, anyway, when she began to write letters — they both went overseas — the little sailor's letters were so much more interesting than the lieutenant's — or whatever he was, I think he was a lieutenant — and she said, "But he's so much more interesting." So she sent the lieutenant the Dear John letter and she married the sailor later on. . . .

There was nothing about birth control in those days. You crossed your fingers, or, like they said, you crossed your legs. Or like I did, I just steered clear. I knew what that meant. As I said, I changed diapers, I knew what that was. I didn't want any of that.

Was abortion ever an option at that time?

No. I don't know if I ever heard the word *abortion* myself. I don't think I heard the word *abortion* even though, on second thought, I guess it was around, because when we were in school some of the people said that some of the girls had gotten pregnant and had abortions. There were some people smarter than we were. I wasn't very smart in that category. But, no, you didn't hear much about abortion except when girls aborted themselves or went to these backstreet things. Oh no, abortion was outlawed and a sin and terrible — so was getting pregnant, let me tell you. A young girl got pregnant, she was an outcast, terrible. . . . There were a lot of girls that got pregnant, but they got married. They were lucky they got married.

Milwaukee had a lot of men from out of town at that time. What were they like?

There were a different kind of men coming in. The first ones were the young guys and they were a lot of fun and they were shy and first time away from home and everything. Now see, [near] the end, they're bringing back the men from the war front and now you're seeing the men with what they call the "fruit salad,". . . all their battle ribbons. . . . So there was a little different feeling now about the USO parties — these were different men and I didn't need these different men, sadly to say. They were in the war, and they were more serious, and they were — well, I had the feeling that they were saying, "Well, you owe me; I fought the war," you know, that. See, I was always a little leery. . . .

[At work there was] a young man that was 4-F, I think, and he was proud of it, I guess. I couldn't understand that either. But, anyway, he was supposed to be doing some work in the office, it was taking care of bills and things. You'd have to pass and make sure this was an honest bill and everything so they would pay it, and you'd just put your okay on it and send it out, and he wasn't doing it. He would just kind of walk around, and I was doing all this stuff. I was getting pretty mad about it because he'd just kind of goof off and I'd end up finishing it so we'd get out. How I discovered that he

*Dorothy and George Zmuda
on Wisconsin Avenue in
Milwaukee, 1945.*

Dorothy Zmuda. WHi(X3)48501

was earning more money than I was, I have no idea. Maybe he told
me, "Well, hey, I earn more than you do."

So, anyway, I went up to [my boss] and I said, "Hey, I'm doing
this fellow's job." And he says, "Well, I know, Dorothy." He says,
"I've tried to get you a raise, but you know." He says, "This is this
time of our life where men earn more than women. They are considered more important, and even if you do the same thing he does and
even if he doesn't even do it, he gets more money than you do, and
this is our world today. Everywhere you go this is what happens."

. . . I said, "Yeah, he just loves work. He can sit there and watch
me do it all day.". . . [My boss] laughed, and then a little while later
I came in and I says, "Ed, [he] didn't show up to work." And he
says, "No, he didn't, Dottie," and he winked a big wink. Got rid of
him — evidently, he got rid of him.

Did you get a raise then?

I don't recall. I don't recall. Probably not. . . . That was one story.
Then another one was, well, I don't know if it was the end of the
year or what, but I found a fur coat. I think it was only $125 at
Gimbel's or Schuster's or somewhere, and was it cute. It was actu-

ally dyed rabbit, but it was cute. It was a little curly thing and I think they had it marked down. So I said, "Hey, I can probably swing this if I pay on it every month," and I bought it. Well, you know that they wouldn't let me have that thing until I — I had a good job and everything — until I went and got my brother's signature. A man had to sign for it, . . . even though I had a job. I had a good job, and I would have paid. And I paid a certain amount down and I would have paid on it. I wouldn't have taken the darn coat home with me until I paid for it. . . . I had to make out a contract, I think it was. My brother had to sign that contract, co-sign it or something. That's how it was for women in those days. Wasn't that the pits? . . .

[After] my other friend Don came home, and one time we went to a Chinese restaurant. . . . There was a long table — you know how they push them together — and bunches of Chinese young men were coming in and sitting at the table and as they started coming in some of them came by and said, "Hi Dottie. Hello Dottie. Oh, this is Dottie — I only heard her on the phone." They were all these young men from Allis-Chalmers. They were training these engineers, and a lot of them were from Allis-Chalmers, and they knew me. Poor Don is sitting there, and he's getting redder. He had just come home from the South Pacific, you know, and I can see him getting redder and redder and madder and madder, and he's getting red and he's gotten mad and I'm watching him. He's watching them and I'm watching him and suddenly he leans over and he says, "Don't tell me you've been dating them goddam son of a bitches," he says. "I just got through killing them two months ago," he says to me. And of course I started to laugh, and I said, "But Don, they're not Japs, they're Chinese." He says, "I don't care. They look the same to me," he says.

3

Women in Uniform

IN ADDITION to providing new opportunities for women in the workplace, the war resulted in the expansion of women's roles in the military. The army already had a tradition of using women as nurses, having established its nurse corps in 1901, and the navy followed suit in 1908. Although more than 10,000 nurses served overseas in World War I, the Second World War saw a tremendous growth in demand for nursing skills. Three out of every ten active professional nurses enlisted, and 76,000 women served in these units, eventually winning full military rank and equal pay.

The employment of women in other military roles generated greater controversy. The shortage of men for noncombat military roles led to the creation of women's units in the U.S. Army (the Women's Auxiliary Army Corps, or WAAC, which later became the Women's Army Corps, WAC), Navy (Women Accepted for Volunteer Emergency Service, or WAVES), the Coast Guard (SPARS, from *Semper Paratus*, or "Always Ready," the Coast Guard motto), and the Marines (women marines). A total of 350,000 women joined these services during World War II, including nearly 6,000 WACs from Wisconsin and another 1,939 women from the state who joined the other services. Most of these women served stateside.

The Red Cross offered another avenue for women to serve in the war. In addition to recruiting women to serve in the Army Nurse Corps and the Navy Nurse Corps, during World War II the Red Cross sent overseas more than 7,000 women and men who ran recreational and medical facilities for military personnel and coordinated relief efforts for civilians and prisoners-of-war in all four theaters of the war (Europe, Africa, the Pacific, and China-Burma-India).

Luida Sanders, Frieda Schurch, Dorothy Keating, Geraldine
Schlosser, and Judy Davenport describe their lives as members of
the women's branches of the military serving in the United States.
Lucille Rabideaux and Signe Cooper relate their experiences as military nurses overseas. Finally, Margaret Kelk and Jane Heinemann,
both of whom eventually served in the Pacific, tell of their tours of
duty as Red Cross recreational workers.

Luida Sanders

Luida Sanders enlisted in the WACs in May, 1943, at the age of twenty-
six. She served as a secretary, as a recruitment officer, and as a hospital
worker, primarily in the southern United States, before leaving the service
at the end of the war.

Why did you join the WACs?

I guess the adventure and the feeling of patriotism. I wanted to be in
it. I'd heard all my life about the relatives that had been in the Civil
War: there were grandfather, great-grandfather, and four great-
uncles all in the Union armies, and we had heard the stories of their
going to war for years. My dad had been at the wrong age at each
war. Whenever there was a war he was either too young or too old
so he was never in, which he regretted, I think. I just wanted to be
in, just wanted to be a part of it. . . .

As soon as I read about the women in uniform, I wanted to be
with them, I really did. My first intention was to join the navy. I
went down to Green Bay, made a special trip, walked into the
recruiting office and asked for information. There were two men
there, and they just laughed and handed me a pamphlet or something and then went off. And I was so embarrassed I walked out
[and] went home and cried. And then I wrote to the army recruiter
in Milwaukee and I got the information from the army. Sent in my
forms that I needed that they sent me. Was called down for physi-
cals and testing. There's no question that I could get in. That was in
May. Decided right then and there. I didn't take it home and think
it over overnight or anything. I just said, "I'm going to do it," and
was sworn in that day. . . . I think the people at church were the
ones who commented most, and for some of them it was, "How can
you leave your mother alone? How can you do that?"

Were the WACs all from similar backgrounds?

In the group that I went in, there were very similar backgrounds.
There were some factory workers and farm girls and city girls, and

clerks and typists. There was a mix. But in particular when I got to Fort Devens, over half of our company were teachers or librarians.

Single?

Most of them, not all. Some were married. Some had husbands in the service. The oldest lady in our company when we got to Fort Devens, she had just barely met the upper age limit — I think it was fifty at the time, I've forgotten — already had grandchildren. One of the highlights of the training sessions was [that] Eleanor Roosevelt was supposed to visit the camp and then it turned out that she didn't have time, really, to get on the ground and go around, so they had us all line up and her airplane flew over and we all waved. But in the meantime, before they found out she wasn't going to come, we policed that area and it was unbelievable. The whole camp, it was absolutely spick-and-span. They even rewhitewashed the stones along the path, picked up everything. The barracks were absolutely spotless. But that was funny — take off our hats and wave them at Eleanor.

What was the training like at Fort Devens? What sort of things did you have to do?

I think it was typical army. They got us up early, and we'd get out and have some report, all line up and then march to mess and then we had classes, we had drill, KP, policed the area. March us back to the mess hall for noon and then classes all afternoon, more drill, physical exercise. My company had their exercise just before mess at night. There wasn't space enough, apparently, for all the companies to do it all at the same time so it would depend [on] which company you were in when you had your physical exercise; we had it just before mess, and we had to be in uniform in order to eat mess, and we had about five minutes, ten minutes, something like that. So we'd dash back, shedding our exercise clothes on the way, dash into the shower, get dressed, then fall out for mess, tying your tie while you were doing it. Then right after mess you were free to go unless you were on special duty of some kind, free to go up to the PX or the service club, USO or whatever. And so, of course, we all tried to be completely dressed so we could leave right after we got through eating, which made it really hurried. . . . I found it exciting, though.

Luida Sanders, 1943.

Courtesy Luida Sanders, WHi(X3)47073

How strenuous was the exercise that the army made women do at the time?

I'll tell you, the first two or three days you just could hardly get through it. In fact, I still have a book, I think, somewhere about the exercise for women. . . . We were supposed to do push-ups. I never did get to do a push-up, never — I always failed that test, always. Until, when I lived in Madison I bought a house that was on a three-quarter-acre lot and I pushed a lawn mower, and one day I discovered I could do push-ups, but in the army I always failed that test.

Do you think fitness was the primary goal of the basic training for women?

It was fitness, for one thing, and then learning to drill. I enjoyed marching and drilling, I really did. And then learn army protocol. Map reading, I remember map reading. Then we had classes in recognizing airplanes so that if we saw an airplane that was an enemy airplane we'd know what to do. I'm afraid I was never terribly good at that, and they'd show the outline of the plane, and you were supposed to say what it was.

What did the WACs hope to do during the course of the war?

One of the big selling points was to relieve a man for active duty. . . . I was assigned to payroll and [when] one of the men there went overseas, I took his job. About a year later, I was in Birmingham and met him, and he said, "Thanks for letting me go." So I felt that I had indeed relieved a man for active duty because I knew that he had gone overseas. There was a lot of paperwork in the army, but to have men sit there doing it when they were needed to fight, why, that was a big selling point — to relieve a man for active duty.

How long did you stay at Fort Devens?

I was just there from June until in August, early August. Just after we were sworn into the WAC and then we were all assigned to posts. I was sent to Fort McClellan, which was an infantry training base at the time, . . . and we were sent to headquarters to do the payroll and the records and that sort of thing. We were basically secretaries and typists and clerks. [In] the groups that I was sent with quite a few of the girls went to mechanic school and became bus drivers and that sort of thing. . . . At Fort McClellan, we were the headquarters company. They had had some officers there and a first sergeant. Oh, ten or twelve women had preceded us, but I was in the first company actually to be assigned there, and that was an experience, it really was. We would be walking down the road and the fellows would be drilling, and the officers would stop them and everybody watched us, saluted. Wherever we appeared there was somebody to watch us. I found it exciting. I really did. . . .

[We] worked from eight until, oh, let's see, I would say six. Not sure if it was five or six but it was six days a week. Reported at eight in the morning. Got up at six, and the first couple of months we were there they had us out drilling every morning and counting cadence, and we managed to count cadence in front of every officers' quarters where they were sleeping, and we counted loud. And then they kind of drifted away from that after a while. But at first they were so protective of the WACs. We had to be so army. We had to drill. You always had to wear your tie, and you always had to have your cap. You always had to be dressed up, and if you went away from the barracks you had to be dressed up, too. If you just stayed around the barracks then you could put on your fatigues and relax, but hardly any of us did. Since it was an infantry training base, [the men] were there for nineteen weeks before they went overseas. . . . They had as many as 40,000 men on the post at any given time, so there was a lot of dating.

*   *   *   *   *

Frieda Schurch

Born to Swiss immigrants in Dodgeville in 1919, Frieda Schurch grew up on the family's farm in Barneveld, in southwestern Wisconsin. After graduating from high school, she attended the University of Wisconsin in 1938-1939 but then returned home to help care for her ailing mother. Following her mother's death in September, 1940, Schurch served as housekeeper for the family's large farm until she joined the WAAC in January, 1943. She remained in the service during the transition to the WAC and was stationed primarily in Des Moines, Iowa, Denton, Texas, and Tampa, Florida, until her discharge in December, 1945. She returned to school, receiving a degree in early childhood development from the University of Wisconsin in 1950, and taught kindergarten in Kenosha from 1952 until 1984. She remains active in politics and still lives in Kenosha.

What prompted you to join the WAACs?

I decided that there was just no future on the farm as a housekeeper and I wasn't being accepted as a partner because the farmers were the partners, [and] I was the housekeeper. When I read about the WAACs, [it] fascinated me.

How did you find out about the WAACs?

We always had a newspaper and often got another Sunday paper. It was always stressed [that] we had to read what was going on; we had to know what was going on in the world and the community. My folks were adults when they came to this country, but they wanted us always to know what was going on. And so of course there were articles on the WAACs in those newspapers, and I decided that was a great thing for me and was a good way of getting out, because I really didn't know when I was ever going to get back to college. I came home to take care of my mother and my mother had died, but now that evolved into being the housekeeper and now I wanted to see an end, going back to school, but I didn't see it. . . . So I simply drove the car to Barneveld and saw a doctor, who had to sign that I was in good health, and then I sent the papers in.

Did your father know anything about this?

Not especially, but a little, but not especially much, no. Then I told him what I'd done when papers came and said I was to go to Milwaukee for two days. My dad wasn't sure how he felt, but he did not object to my brother taking me to Barneveld. We lived four miles out, so I had to be taken to the train station and he did take me, and there was no problem there.

What was their reaction? Were they surprised?

Yes, and kind of disappointed. But my brother took me to the train station, my dad had no objection to that. . . . I had my physical, had my exams and the psychologist talked to you, but you also had some written exams and then you were sworn in actually and then taken back to the depot.

What was the trip to Milwaukee like?

A lot of people there and we were all anxious to go to the service and we were very different. Each had a roommate and I guess I'm an outgoing person, and so I was interested in talking to all these people and finding out what their interests were, who they were and what they did and how they felt about going in the service. You got more enthusiastic — there were a lot of people around.

. . . And then I got a notice to report January 24, 1943. My dad said, "Write and tell them you can't come now." And I said, "No, this is what I want to do." He even put some money in the bank for me in case I needed to come home because he knew I didn't have any. He was a very practical person.

What was his reaction after you returned from your induction in Milwaukee?

I think he kind of thought I would back out. I think he thought he shouldn't stop me, but he had, I think, strong hopes then that I'd had enough when I would go to Milwaukee. But only it just increased me.

How did the rest of your family react?

My brother, of course, was disappointed [that] I left. Only my one brother was home, the other was on [another] farm. My sister-in-law and my sisters, of course, were very supportive of what I was doing. I wouldn't say that my brother at home really tried to keep me from going, but he was disappointed that I was going.

Frieda Schurch at Drew Field, Tampa, Florida, 1945.

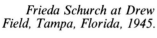

Courtesy Frieda Schurch. WHi(X3)48542

Did he let you know that?

You could tell, you knew it. Because after all, to live on a farm without a housekeeper is bad business. The neighbors even reminded me of that.

How did the army treat the WAACs?

Drew Field [in Tampa] was run by regular army people, and regular army people did not want women on the base, . . . so they put us five miles out, off the base, in a swamp area that wasn't drained and had mosquitoes. They had built four barracks and a mess hall. And then we had a bus that came every morning and came every night, and you better get out there at five, and you were supposed to work until five so you had to run. Every night at five it rained and so you ran through the rain and got in the bus and went to the barracks. . . .

We were not a hundred WAACs at the base, but we always averaged fourteen in the hospital for infected mosquito bites. And I came home once during that time, and my legs react to mosquito bites, but otherwise mosquitoes can land on my arm and I don't react. In those days it took forty-four hours on the train to get from Tampa Field to Barneveld, . . . and if I sit up that long then my legs swell, and between the swelling of my legs and all those mosquito bites, my dad looked at my legs and said, "Is that what you went in the service for?" He said, "You'd never have those kind of legs at home, and you wouldn't have them now."

But, anyway, we were then discharged [during the transition from the WAAC to WAC], and there were two women who were a little older, had been around a little more than me, that's for sure, and were from the New York City area and they had a little money and they simply got out of the service. . . . [They] took a place on the beach at St. Petersburg, which was near Tampa, and then they could write directly to Washington, D.C. You didn't have to go through any chain anymore, and [they] told them what conditions we were living under in Tampa, Florida, Drew Field, and then we were moved out of there. . . . Then later, as time went on, [the army] decided that area was built up and they could use that for the German war prisoners, but it did not pass the Geneva Accord and so it had to be drained, because of the mosquitoes. But we lived under [those conditions]. See, we were not part of the army then, we were WAAC, and the old army was in charge of the base, and they always made rulings that exempted the women [from equal treatment].

Did you expect this sort of treatment when you joined the military?

I didn't think it was right, but it wasn't so over-shocking and you just kept fighting it. . . . The officer of the headquarters called all the WAACs who worked at headquarters back from seven to ten [in the evening], Monday, Wednesday, and Friday to work, but [he] had everything locked up so there was no work. And because then you're more apt to break, if there's nothing to do. If they had come back, he figured, every night, and there was really emergency things to do, we would never break. But he had hopes that by calling those women back Monday, Wednesday, and Friday and having nothing to do from seven to ten [when] they had to be there . . . that they would break. But they didn't.

What do you mean by "break?"

I mean a breakdown, a mental breakdown, a nervous breakdown [is] what it was called then. Yes, that's what they thought they could do. Then they'd be discharged for Section 8, which was not a good discharge, especially not then. . . .

After the POWs came, [to prevent fraternization,] we closed our mess hall because the German prisoners did the KP, . . . and we all ate with the men. And this one day this woman was in the line and as she went ahead, the man ahead of her stepped back, which can happen because he passed something and decided he wanted it. It was nothing mean, but they collided, and so her tray flew to the floor and there was a German war prisoner standing there with a mop and he came right over to clean up and he picked up the tray and handed it to her and she said, "Thank you," and the mess sergeant wanted her court-martialed for talking to a German war prisoner. And that went on for a while before it was thrown out. And our commanding officer said that every week she got a call, and the rumors and the stories got worse, [like] she was pregnant from the German war prisoner, to that extent, and therefore she needed to be court-martialed. And all that had happened actually was when she was handed that tray she said, "Thank you."

*   *   *   *   *

Dorothy Keating
Dorothy (Doxtator) Keating, a full-blooded Oneida Indian, was born in Laona, in Forest County, in 1924. She grew up in a series of foster homes and government boarding schools. Keating joined her mother in Milwaukee in the summer of 1942, after her junior year of high school. Rather than returning to school, Keating got a job making circuit breakers at Cutler-Hammer and later worked at Allis-Chalmers as a coil winder. She joined the WAVES in 1944 and served as a pharmacist mate, second class, for two and a half years, working in Maryland, Oklahoma, and New York. Keating has been married three times, most recently to Thomas Keating, who died in 1990. She worked for the Stockbridge-Munsee Indian tribe for almost ten years until her retirement in 1990, and she earned her high school general equivalency diploma in 1982. She received an associate degree in social work from the University of Wisconsin-Stevens Point in 1985. She currently lives on the Stockbridge-Munsee Reservation in Shawano County.

How did your mother react when you told her that you were thinking about joining the military?

She felt bad at first because I already had four brothers in the service, and she didn't want me to go at first. But when she saw how badly I wanted to go — this was in between the time that I had signed up and the time when I got the letter — but when I got the letter and she read it and it was so impressive. When the government sends you a letter, "We want to welcome you," your family is willing to release you to serve your country and things like that. The

Courtesy Dorothy Keating. WHi(X3)48261

Dorothy Keating (front row, last woman on right) with her WAVES unit, ca. 1944-45.

letter was so impressive. She cried, but she just melted then, said, "Well, you've got to go."

How did the military deal with the fact that you were American Indian?

The only thing that really bothered us is that in those days you were either black or white and on many of my documents and things like that that I have, and my discharge papers, I'm considered white. There was no "other," or there was no check for American Indian. There wasn't even red. You were either black or white, and if you were American Indian you were considered white.

What was basic training like for you?

I was pretty much of a tomboy anyway, being the youngest and having four brothers, so being in that type of the training where we had the ropes, the rope training, and getting aboard ship and things like that with the rope ladders, and all the calisthenics and things like that — I just ate that up because it was something that I was used to and I had training in, like I said. I had taken acrobatic training when I was young — like thirteen — and that and calisthenics wasn't much different. You had to do all these different exercises

and everything to keep you in shape and all this running and jumping and all that. Swinging from ropes, all that. I ate it up. I was in
my glory. I excelled at it and it made me feel good because I was one
jump ahead of them. But this was kind of nice, because they'd say,
"Of course she could do it, because she's Indian" — like Indians
were supposed to be very agile.

* * * * *

Geraldine Schlosser

Born in Tomah in 1921, Geraldine (Sowle) Schlosser received her undergraduate education at Milwaukee State Teachers College and the University of Wisconsin. In early 1943, she joined the WAAC, reenlisting in July
in the WAC when the WAAC was disbanded. After basic training she
attended radio school in Newark, New Jersey, and then served as a radio
technician in Midland, Texas, until November, 1945. After the war, she
returned to the University of Wisconsin, where she pursued a graduate
degree in anthropology and met her future husband, James Schlosser. The
couple married in 1947, and the Schlossers moved to Milwaukee, where
Geraldine did general office work until the birth of her first child, in 1952.
She returned to work in 1960 as an interviewer for the University of
Wisconsin Survey Research Laboratory and then attended library school
a few years later, receiving her master's degree from the University of
Wisconsin-Milwaukee in 1968. She was then employed as a librarian at
the Milwaukee Public Library until she and her husband retired and
moved to Tomah in 1982.

What was school in Newark like?

It was a civilian school — United Radio Television Institute. . . .
We lived in a hotel just a block from the railroad station there in
Newark and we marched en masse to our school — it was quite a
few blocks away. It was a good school — I mean, those men knew
how to teach the fundamentals of radio. Another girl that was in
the class went with me out to Midland, there were two of us, and we
weren't really accepted [by the men]. I think they didn't know exactly what to do with us. . . . I think they probably thought that
we didn't know enough. I mean, how could women know anything
about this? I suppose some of them might have felt, "Well, she'll
replace me, and I'll have to go on active duty." Of course, that
didn't really happen, [but] I think there was that feeling among men
in the service.

I never really used all that I learned in radio school because what
we did at Midland was we had to troubleshoot any radio problems.
But instead of actually fixing the radio, we just exchanged units.
When something [was] wrong with the transmitter, you just put a

Mary Trish and Geraldine Schlosser, Midland, Texas, summer, 1943.

Courtesy Geraldine Schlosser. WHi(X3)48288

new one in — took the old one out. I mean you had to be able to figure out what the trouble was. Oh, and we wired antennas on these planes, too. . . .

The thing that really did bother me, though, at Midland was the fact that when we got a Negro detachment in — of WACs — and they could not belong to our squadron. We were Squadron D and they were Squadron G, and they were housed separately, fed separately, and everything. We had one girl who was assigned to our work unit, . . . but that really bothered me that they were segregated that way. And that was before there was very much being said or done about segregation.

*   *   *   *   *

Judy Davenport

Born in 1920, Judy Geraldine (Schamens) Davenport grew up in Leon, near Sparta, and joined the WAACs in November, 1942. She completed basic training in Des Moines, Iowa, and later was stationed in Georgia and Louisiana as a cook. Davenport served for ten months, choosing not to reenlist because of an injury when the WAAC was converted into the WAC in 1943. She returned to Leon, where she married career military officer James Davenport on October 31, 1944. She spent the next four decades raising the couple's four children and doing volunteer work, primarily in the Leon area. Widowed in 1986, she now lives in Sparta.

*Judy Davenport
and her father,
Everett Schamens,
ca. 1943.*

Courtesy Judy Davenport, WHi(X3)48473

[In] Des Moines, Iowa, it was at Christmas time and Eleanor
Roosevelt went through the [mess] line . . . and she said, "Well,
you know, I'd like more potatoes." I says, "You know the rules, get
going." I looked up and there was Eleanor Roosevelt, and she says,
"Well, at least there's one thing, you're doing your job the way you
should." So I said, "Yeah." And that's one thing I said, I got a big
kick out of — I told Eleanor Roosevelt off.

And then when I was in Fort Oglethorpe, we had drill, and President Roosevelt was there. They had him go around with his car and
there was twelve of us girls that passed out because it was 120 [de-
grees] in the shade, see, and we were standing in the sun. So there
was quite a few of us that fell for President Roosevelt. We fell
passed out!

*   *   *   *   *

Lucille Rabideaux

The daughter of Lakota Indian and French parents, Lucille (LeBeau)
Rabideaux was born in Dewey County, South Dakota, in 1914. She
attended Indian schools before enrolling in the Sioux City Methodist
Hospital Nurses School, from which she was graduated in 1938. Rabideaux moved to Wisconsin in 1939 and worked as a nurse for the

Indian Service in Hayward, in Sawyer County. While there, she met
Francis Martin Rabideaux, a Red Cliff Chippewa from Bayfield, on Lake
Superior. They married in 1941, shortly after he was drafted into the
army. In June, 1943, Rabideaux enlisted as an army nurse with the Forty-
fourth General Hospital Unit, based from Madison, and she served in
Australia, New Guinea, and the Philippines before being discharged in
March, 1946. After the war, Francis Rabideaux reenlisted in the army,
and the Rabideaux family followed him to a number of posts in the
United States and abroad before his death in Thailand in 1968. Lucille
Rabideaux then returned to Ashland, where she still lives, and worked as
a nurse until her retirement in 1980.

*How did you feel about going overseas? Did you know how long it
would take?*

No, we didn't know what ship we were going on. You aren't told
anything. We went to Los Angeles. We had to be at a certain place
at a certain time, but they let us go and eat, the last place we could
go and eat in the city. . . . We knew we had to get on our train and
we would be traveling all night up to Pittsburg, California, to Camp
Stoneman. . . . We were there two days; then we had our packs on
our backs and we were in our fatigues. We put cardboard over our
shoulders but we still got sore because we had to march two miles in

*Lucille Rabideaux (left) and
Alyce Rademacker at
Camp Anza, Arlington,
California, 1942.*

Courtesy Lucille Rabideaux. WHi(X3)48253

the heat to the ferries. We got our final orders and our final exam and everything the first day we were there. And then the next day we had to have our bedding rolls, everything all packed and the trucks took everything to where they were going to be loaded on a ship, we didn't know. And then we had to march, it was slow marching, we had two miles to march — Camp Stoneman to where the ferries were going to take us down the bay.

We got there, I guess, just when the sun was setting, it was going to be dark, and they loaded us up on the ferries and it was evening. And it was cold, and they put us on the ferries anyway. We didn't have any wraps. We got down in between the seats so we could get out of the wind. It was really cold, and we went down the bay and we didn't get on the ship, the U.S.S. *West Point*, until eleven o'clock at night. . . . They loaded us up and they gave us a cold supper, a cold tray.

How did enlisted men deal with taking orders from the nurses?

Fine. I only ran into one [problem], when we had a hospital in Australia, and we had a black patient, and so I gave [a corpsman] the medicine to give. It was on night duty, and I give him the medicine, it was pain medication, I guess, to take to this black man — sol-

Courtesy Lucille Rabideaux. WHi(X3)48321
The orthopedic ward at the Forty-fourth General Hospital, north of Townsville, Australia, ca. 1944.

dier — and he refused. So I told him, "There's no Mason-Dixon line in the army. I'm giving you an order. You take this medicine to that man, or I'm going to write you up." So he took it, and I went and I watched him, and he gave the medicine. And he said, "You nigger lover," and I said, "You bet, you bet I am." So he didn't make any more fuss about it because he knew I meant what I said. So I didn't have any more trouble with him.

Were there ever any black nurses serving in your unit?

Not in our unit, but there was a contingent of degree nurses from the South . . . and if there was a couple of them at our table, some white nurses wouldn't fill it; they'd go to start the next table. And the officer who was in charge of the mess hall, when they started to serve, he announced, . . . "The tables will be filled just like you are in line." And so that stopped, but those southern whites would not sit at the table with them. [It] didn't make any difference to me. [The black nurses] were nice.

*   *   *   *   *

Signe Cooper
 Born in Clinton County, Iowa, in 1921, Signe (Skott) Cooper moved with her family to McFarland, just outside Madison, in 1937. Cooper was graduated from the University of Wisconsin's nursing school in 1943. She joined the Army Nurse Corps in May, 1943, and was stationed at Fort Belvoir in northern Virginia, just outside of the District of Columbia, from May, 1943, to August, 1944, when she was sent to the China-Burma-India (CBI) theater. There, she worked in a hospital on the Ledo Road, a route running from Ledo, in the Indian province of Assam, through Burma into southern China. She spent the duration of the war in India, moving to Burma for a month after the war ended. After her discharge at the end of 1945, she returned to Madison, where she worked at Wisconsin General Hospital (now the University of Wisconsin Hospital) and later became a professor of nursing at the university. She retired in 1983 and now lives in the Madison suburb of Middleton.

What kind of army training did you receive?

When I went into the service there wasn't such a thing as basic training for nurses [although] there was shortly afterwards. Almost anybody who went in later went to Camp McCoy for three months of basic training. The only kind of basic training that we got was occasionally we would do some drilling. After a full day of duty we'd go out on the drill field and do some drilling and every so often they'd show us films and things. That was the kind of training that we got. Mostly we learned from other people. We'd start out working with the experienced people and that was the kind of on-the-job training that we got. . . .

We were in New York for two weeks before we were sent overseas. While we were in New York we marched around. The person who was in charge of us had us march every day in Central Park. So we'd march around in Central Park. They would line us up from the tallest to the shortest, and one of my friends and I were the tallest, so she and I — we marched two by two — were always at the head of the count. If she was out of step she never could get in step so the rest of us would have to change to get in step. I can remember marching around Central Park — I know it was only two weeks, but it seemed like months. Every morning we'd get up and we'd march around Central Park. People would sort of look at us and sort of laugh at us, and there we were marching around in Central Park. I don't suppose it would even be safe to do that now.

What was a typical day like in India?

My average workday, for the most part, was only six hours because most of the time I opted for night duty because it was so terribly hot and most people couldn't sleep. Night duty was either seven o'clock to one o'clock or one o'clock to seven o'clock. I very often opted for one of those tours of duty because everybody else was reluctant to take it and I didn't have too much trouble sleeping even when it was awful hot. . . . Otherwise, the tour of duty was from seven o'clock to four o'clock or seven o'clock to twelve o'clock and four o'clock to seven o'clock. Most of the time we had split shifts. I did an awful lot of night duty when I was in India.

My most favorite experience — and it probably wasn't for longer than a month or two — was on the scrub typhus unit. That was because those patients really needed good nursing care. There wasn't much that could be done for them. This was before antibiotics. The casualty rate actually was very high. They were using a drug — this is hard to believe, I guess — it was called para-aminobenzoic acid, PABA, [and] it's now the active ingredient in suntan lotions, but they were using it with some success in the treatment of scrub typhus. Oh my, those memories still stick.

Interestingly enough, when I went to the psych wards — and the reason I was sent to the psych wards was because I'd had it as a student nurse and at that time it wasn't a requirement in nursing programs so a lot of the nurses had not had experience in psychiatric nursing — so they sent me to the psych ward. . . . And a lot of the patients who did survive the scrub typhus and were sent back to

Courtesy Lucille Rabideaux. WHi(X3)48322

The Forty-fourth General Hospital operating as an evacuation hospital at Dulag on Leyte, Philippines, 1944.

duty I would often see again because they would eventually come back to the psych wards because their attitude was [that] they survived scrub typhus, [so the military] shouldn't have sent [them] back to duty, and there was some logic to what they said. So, anyway, we would see a lot of those patients because eventually they would land back on the psych wards. We had a very interesting experience.

Were there a lot of people who didn't survive the scrub typhus unit?

We averaged a casualty a day. It was unbelievable, it was unbelievable. It was caused by a mite. When the fellows would go out in the jungles — sort of like Lyme disease today, if you go out in the woods, it's risky — that's what would happen. They would get bit, and you could also find where they had been bitten by this mite. So sick — very high fever, very often irrational. But it was a good nursing experience. You really felt like you were doing something when you were taking care of those fellows.

Tell me something about the type of accommodations you lived in.

We lived in — we called them bashas, and they had concrete floors, and the sides of the building were woven reeds. This was all handmade by Indian labor. Corrugated iron roofs that was thatched over and two of us lived in a room. The basha that I lived in, there were eight of us, but that was the smallest one; usually they were larger. Each adjoining room had a little kind of an anteroom in the back where it had a little sink, and that's where we made tea or brushed our teeth or whatever. The water was polluted, so all our drinking water and toothbrushing water, things like that, we had to get from a Lister bag. They were big canvas bags — I don't even know what they put in it, iodine or something — but it tasted terrible, but at least you knew you weren't drinking polluted water. Once in a long while, a very long while, we would even get ice — I don't know where we got this, probably in the bazaar at Margarita, which was not very far away — we would crank out ice cream made with bananas and Pet milk. It sounds terrible, but at the time it was wonderful. We were warned against eating local fruits and vegetables, [although there were some exceptions,] like apples you could soak in potassium permanganate to sterilize them, [and] the bananas were okay because you could just take the peel off of them and they were okay.

Courtesy Signe Cooper. WHi(X3)48518

Signe Cooper (right) in front of a basha in Assam, India, ca. 1944-45.

What else would you do while you were there? Were there dances or USO shows coming through or things like that?

We didn't get very many shows. We were really at the end of the earth. Some that I remember, I remember Pat O'Brien and Jinx Falkenberg did come to our part of the world, and Louis Armstrong came. And that's absolutely the only celebrities that I can remember at all. We had some of our own home-grown entertainment occasionally. We did have a lot of movies. You could practically go to the movie, I think, every night if you wanted to, and occasionally they would start classes like, well, I remember writing class. Only, what would happen — these would be convalescent people that would be teaching, and they'd go back to their units, so that would end after about three or four days or something.

I did a lot of reading. I've always been a reader. . . . Somebody in our basha bought a phonograph. We couldn't get very many records, though, and she would play the records over and over. We had occasional parties and dances and things like that, but not a lot. . . . We also had the feeling that nobody knew where we were and that nobody cared. In fact, the nurses that I knew who were in Europe — this was after Roosevelt had died — they used to sing a song about "Dear Mr. Truman, please let me go home," and one of the lines was "But don't send I to the CBI," which when we heard about it we sort of laughed because everybody felt like the CBI was the end of the earth.

How did the duties assigned to the women in the Army Nurse Corps change as a result of the hardships you endured?

I think the role of the nurse changed after World War II because I think that many of the nurses who served in the army were not willing to subject themselves to some of the kinds of subservience, I guess, that had been evident before that. I, myself, never felt so much of that because in the university program we didn't have as much of that as the kind of stories that people would tell me about what happened to them when they were in training — those kinds of things. I never cleaned any doctor's shoes and stuff like that — that was never a part of our experience here. But I think after the war . . . nurses did not accept the kind of subservient role that they had in some places. I think they were given a lot more responsibilities. They were very often essentially on their own. I think there were many, many changes, some subtle and some not so subtle. But I think the experience of war really made a difference to nursing.

The other important thing is that many of us took advantage of the
GI Bill of Rights and got more education and I think that made a
difference to nursing too.

*Did the nurses act almost as an unofficial support group for each
other?*

I think we did. The words are new, of course, but I think we did. I
think some of those experiences that we had we probably wouldn't
have survived without sort of helping each other through it. I think
we were very much a support group for each other, even though we
didn't call it that. It's like we didn't talk about culture shock, but we
had culture shock.

*   *   *   *   *

Margaret Kelk

Born in 1917 in Rhinelander, Margaret (Ebert) Kelk grew up in Lake
Tomahawk, where her parents operated a girls' camp. She received a
degree in education from the University of Wisconsin in 1939. During her
last two years of college, she worked part-time for the *Wisconsin State
Journal,* moving to full-time work in the advertising department after
graduating. Following the attack on Pearl Harbor, she took a secretarial
position with the Badger Ordnance plant in Baraboo, where she worked
until she joined the American Red Cross Military Welfare Service in
September, 1943. Kelk received two weeks of training in Washington,
D.C., before she was shipped to the Pacific theater, where she served in New
Caledonia, Guadalcanal, and Hawaii. Her only brother, Mark Johnson
Ebert, who was eighteen months her junior, was killed on a bombing
mission over Bucharest, Romania, on April 4, 1944. After the war, she
returned to Wisconsin, where she taught English and social studies at the
junior high level at several Wisconsin schools from 1946 until her marriage to Harry Kelk in 1955. Since that time, she has owned and operated
a summer campground trailer park in Lake Tomahawk. Her husband
died in 1988.

They were pushing girls to go into the service — the WACs, the
WAVES, the marines were in the plant trying to recruit people for
service. It was push, push, push, and we were all interviewed for
this, and [they] said, "Won't you please join up? We need people in
service." . . . So I wasn't crazy about the services, and I found out
the American Red Cross was going after people and I tried that
and, bang, I was into that.

Why did you choose the Red Cross rather than the services?

Well, my brother was drafted and I thought I had more leeway as a
civilian working with the army than I would be if I was drafted as
another service person. And — oh, this is kind of strange — the

American Red Cross had the reputation of only taking the cream of the crop, which is of course a lot of baloney because you get a cross-section of American personalities no matter where you are. "But, oh, if you could get in the Red Cross, that was way above the services. That was just the scum you see, they'll take anybody, but you have to be special to get in the Red Cross. Okay, give it a whirl." And I did. And they send you to Washington, D.C., for two weeks of training in what they want you to do, and I did that. . . . Nobody in the area was going into the Red Cross. They were all just going into service as WACs, WAVES, or marine girls. But that was anybody — high school graduates could go into that, but they were only taking college graduates in the Red Cross, that was one thing, and I had the degree.

Do you know why they required a college education?

No. It was supposedly a highbrow thing. And you got paid differently. Of course, you are still a civilian working with the army, and I thought I might be able to choose where I went, and, by golly, I was going to go over to Italy, where my brother landed. But I made the mistake of telling somebody that, and so they sent me in the opposite direction because they're not going to listen to that.

What did the training in Washington involve?

Mostly they said, "You are to take care of the enlisted man. He is the one who is facing the guns and fighting the war. You have officer status" — we were officer status — "but do not fall into the habit of being in officers' clubs or with officers." I found out when I got into the service that the enlisted man felt bad about his situation and he did not have good communication with the officer class. Except for the air corps, there was a very definite division. And they said, "Take care of the enlisted man and do not have a special thing that you must do because recreation is what anybody wants. If he wants to read, give him reading materials." The Red Cross gave us a lot of stuff in small little editions. We even got newspapers that were [shrunk]. *Time* magazine was [about six inches high]. "Or if he wants to talk, listen to him. If he's upset, try to think what you can do. Organize the men into skits, little plays, little drama things."

Did they have you practice such things during your training?

No, they just showed us how it could work and gave us just a lot of ways in which we could be very, very helpful. They said, "When you go into a station, you may have to set up a place where you can do these things. Now, you work with the army." They showed us how to work with the army. "You must always obey the army. You cannot ever double-cross them. But, on the side, if the army cannot provide you with what you want, then you are a civilian; you may go out and talk to the navy or someplace else. You need a can of paint and the army hasn't got it, find the navy; they've always got paint." And this went on and on and we got to be very clever with it. We could moonlight, we had rights, things that we could do that army personnel could not do.

It sounds like they gave you a lot of flexibility.

They did, and that was where the fun part came in, a lot of it. And we could thumb our noses at the army once in a while, [but you] can't take it too far.

Did you know from the time you arrived in Washington where you were going to be sent?

We never knew where we were going to be sent. When we got on the train, we didn't know which direction we were going in. We were going west — we finally found that out when we got to San Fran-

Margaret Kelk,
New Caledonia, ca.
June-December,
1944.

Courtesy Margaret Kelk. WHi(X3)48520

cisco. Nobody in the group [knew], and I think there were forty Red Cross people, and we had absolutely no idea.

Why do you suppose that was?

They didn't want the information out where the shipping or where anything was going. We ended up on a troopship, you see. There were thousands of men on that trip. Two of them died in a hold from — see, it was crowded, very, very crowded — heat exhaustion, and it was just jammed with troops. And even when we were on the ocean — we didn't see land for two weeks — and during that time we had no idea where we were going. And finally, about halfway over there, I think we crossed the equator, and I had had the sense enough to take a world map with me and everybody was borrowing it wondering where we were going to land and finally the news came through, somewhere about a week later, ten days, that we were going to Noumea, New Caledonia. That's where the ship was bound for. They just didn't want the information out in any way. Well, they were afraid of Japanese submarines or intelligence. There was plenty of that.

So this was a general training program?

Yes. Every Red Cross girl worked under a Red Cross director who was, as far as I know, a man. Except that up the hierarchy there were women, for instance, stationed in the Pacific theater and Hawaii who kind of branched, had some fingers out. It was very well organized. I thought it was beautifully organized. Wherever you were stationed there was a Red Cross man [and] nine-tenths of his job was to communicate with the army. And if you had a soldier in trouble or a family back home in trouble, then he was the communication through the Red Cross as to what could be done for him or should he be sent home on an emergency and that kind of thing. And he did a lot of book work on that and did a lot of that kind of [thing] — we did none of that. All we did was an entertainment sort of thing.

But I did teach a class of illiterates for a while — soldiers who couldn't read or write. Anything that they needed, the GI, [the Red Cross] said, "Take care of the GI, take care of the GI. What he needs, do for him, and don't let the officers try and swing you off in their direction," which they were always trying to do. A lot of pressure there.

What were you told about your role with the soldiers? Were you warned about getting too close to them?

The only thing that I recall is that we would be with people of different religions, different backgrounds, and it would be better not to get personally involved with anyone. But of course you cannot control that. Some girls did [get involved]. I did not, as it turned out. Very few of the girls that I knew got into this officer thing. When we went to Noumea one day the Red Cross man who was in charge of the Noumea district came to me and he said, "General Nimitz is here, and there's going to be a big party" — General Nimitz is the [admiral in charge of the Pacific naval campaign] — "and he wants a lady escort, and we picked you for it, and he knows who you are and he would like to have you be his escort." And I said, "No way. Forget it fast. I will not even consider it." Because every time a Red Cross girl fell into that little mess, the GIs turned against her because there was this very different division — officers, GIs. It is not like your movie of M*A*S*H, not quite, and you had officers' clubs. I never went to an officers' club. I never dated officers and you had plenty of chances to, believe me. And I'll never forget, even in the Twenty-fifth Division, which is a fighting group and your of-

Courtesy Margaret Kelk. WHi(X3)48519

Margaret Kelk (center, in striped shirt) with American troops and other recreation workers in New Caledonia, ca. June-December, 1944.

ficers had better behave themselves because if you're in a group where an officer gets out of line and then you get into battle, the officer is the first one who gets shot by your own men. And this did happen. Plenty of times. I heard about it. But, I had to eat — I could not eat with the GIs. I had to eat in the officers' club — all of us did. Why? I don't know, I don't know. . . .

[On Guadalcanal, there] was just a very small unit of men and it was a mixed unit. There weren't very many of these blacks and whites, and I had no prejudice. So I remember organizing — we were going to have a beach party and I got to the mess hall and I got some hampers of sandwiches and junk and we got a couple of beach balls and I took the men — not all of them went, but the men who wanted to go — and we went down to the beach. We went swimming and played on the beach and had a bonfire and ate, but there were black men and white men. Didn't bother me any, I wasn't supposed to be bothered. Got back to the unit, nothing was said, we had a wonderful time.

The next day I was taken back to headquarters, where I stayed with all the other girls, then the jeep took me back the next day and the Red Cross man had gone to headquarters and had me fired. That was to be my last day. I said, "What?" Because I had been out with the black men on the beach — there was this division between blacks and whites then . . . He was a bigoted person, and what happened to him, I don't know. But he went to the Red Cross and he insisted that I was not to be there and the Red Cross went to the army, and so I don't know how it happened. All I know is that I was not to be there anymore because of this reason and the sergeant, the top sergeant of the unit, was in his office when I got there and he bawled him out all afternoon. . . . He just gave him the worst hell you ever heard. He just told him off right and left. He was so mad at him for doing this. He said, "That's what we want, that's what we need." . . .

I was still in Guadalcanal when [the Americans retook the Philippines] and they were shipping the people who had been prisoners there out, and this one girl . . . who had been a prisoner there was staying with us. She was in her early twenties — I think she was a few years younger than I was — and she looked like sixty years old. She had dark circles clear down here, and she said — she was on her way home but she just stayed with us overnight, somehow she was getting transportation — she said, "We in America will never ever know what trouble is. When the Philippine [people] kill their own children to keep them from being captured by the Japanese," she said, "That's what I saw." Oh, I'll never forget that. I get emotional, too, to this day. . . .

Hawaii was interesting because we ran a canteen on Hickam Field. See, the planes were coming in and bringing the GIs home who had been out there by the planeload-full, and they'd land all night long. And we had the night shift and then the Red Cross women volunteers took care of it during the day and all night long we'd serve — they'd get off the plane and come on the field, on the airfield, and here we were set up for them for coffee and doughnuts and sliced pineapple, and I guess we served pineapple juice, too. I can't remember. I remember slicing pineapple all night long and making coffee all night long. The doughnuts were made for us, we didn't have to cook. They were so happy to see American [women], to have this before they had to go in and find their unit. . . .

What about the food when you were in the Pacific?

All the girls in the Red Cross complained about it except me. I'd lived through the depression and any food, any nourishment was fine. I mean, I just have never been a fussy person anyway. This one girl, oh my goodness. Well, she'd come from a very rich family and she was an awful nice girl and she did a good job but she, "Oh, the food." So she lost all this weight and she wouldn't eat and all that stuff, and I can't remember that there was anything to complain about really. Of course, the story was the American GI was overfed, overpaid, and oversexed. You heard that one before. I think they did all right. It wasn't always elegant and it was always the same and sometimes you had GI rations, but so what? It's good food. If you got terribly tired of it and you could get down into Noumea or into some French village where the French were trying to serve up a restaurant, you could get sea fish, oysters and — if you got steak and eggs, oh boy, that was the greatest.

What was it like to have a brother in the service and to be working with other servicemen?

I was thinking of them as my brother. I was trying to do for them what I was hoping somebody would do for my brother. My brother was not a fighting man. When he was drafted, he was sent immediately to — well, he was supposed to go to Annapolis and then he went to a physical and his blood pressure was high that day, so he was discredited. So then he was supposed to go to officers' training and they lost all his records so then he had to go to another place, in the United States this was, and they lost his records again. I don't know how this could happen, but it can. So then he was down in Arizona and they made him drill sergeant for a while and then the pressure — air force, air force, air force, go, go, go. He was sick of being drill sergeant and the pay was big [in the air force] and he called me up and he said, "I'm going," and he said, "I might not come back," and [he] didn't. [It was a] hard telephone call. I was in Hercules Powder Company then [before joining the Red Cross], and I was bound and determined I was going to get over there. But I treated the other men as I would have him. But for years I used to break up over him.

* * * * *

Jane Heinemann

Born in Wausau in 1917 and raised in Merrill, Jane Heinemann received a bachelor's degree in music education from Northwestern University in 1940 and taught music in schools in Earlville, Illinois, and Hammond, Indiana. She joined the Red Cross in 1943 and was sent to Camp Chaffee, Arkansas, an armored training post, where she became a staff recreation worker, charged with entertaining recovering GIs in the station hospital. The Red Cross sent her to the western Pacific in 1945. She first went to Tinian, in the Mariana Islands, with one of five hospitals to be set up for the planned invasion of Japan. Heinemann remained overseas after the war ended and moved to club service on Guam and Saipan. She returned to the United States in early 1946, but later that year the Red Cross called her back to William Beaumont General Hospital, in El Paso, Texas, where she worked with long-term battle casualties. She returned to teaching in Michigan, Wisconsin, Illinois, Arizona, Maryland, and Iowa over the next five years before joining the U.S. Army's Special Services and becoming a program director in GI service clubs in Germany during 1953 and 1954. She returned to Wisconsin in 1954 and taught music at the University of Wisconsin-Milwaukee until her retirement in 1986. She now resides in the Milwaukee suburb of Glendale.

A boy named Joe had been laying mines [during] training — real ones — and one had gone off and mangled part of one arm and blinded and deafened him. I first saw him on the surgical ward when I just happened to be there on a routine visit. He was in the private room and he had had surgery — I think they removed part of his arm — and he had not yet gone into shock and so he was quite talkative.

The next time I saw him he had been moved to the locked [psychiatric] ward in the private room and he looked like a mummy, he was all strapped up. He couldn't see me. . . . I didn't think he was conscious. I went back to the day room with my rolling piano and we were singing, and the nurse came back to say that Joe would like to hear a rumba, and I couldn't think of a rumba, so I played "Be-

*Jane Heinemann playing the accordian at the 915th Aircraft Engineers
Battalion Club on Guam, 1945.*

gin the Beguine" and something else Spanish. Then when I left I
stopped in to talk to Joe and here he was with the stump of his arm
on a board strapped to the wall and looking like a mummy, but he
could talk and he could hear some, and he thanked me. He said that
was the best shot in the arm he'd had since he was in the hospital.
This was the one time when I started to cry, but he couldn't see it.
And then he asked me if I liked strawberry malts, and of course I
said I did, and he said he would ask his sisters to get me one at the
PX — they had been called from Chicago when he was on the critical list. Well, he remembered, and we went to the PX, and they
bought me a strawberry malt, and I drank it and cried again.

Well, I saw Joe sometimes after that and he went to several general hospitals. He had been a Boy Scout and a leader in northern
Wisconsin. My father had been in scout work too, so my father
wrote to him. And in the meantime I went overseas and when I
came back I went to Northwestern to start my master's and I heard
that Joe was engaged to a girl in Chicago. They were furnishing an
apartment, so I went to the apartment and I saw Joe, really for the
first time, and Carol, his fiancée. Then I found out that he was convinced that "Begin the Beguine" had saved his life by pulling him
out of shock because they hadn't been able to get him out. And on
his chart — and of course the GIs just love to read their charts —
on his chart for the past three nights it had said, "Patient not ex-
pected to live through the night," and so he thought "Begin the
Beguine" had done it, and Carol was convinced, too. . . .

[Years later,] I was at a convention in Eau Claire, so I went to
visit them in Chippewa Falls, and I drove up and here was a sixteen-
year-old waiting at the curb, and he shook my hand and said,
"You're Jane Heinemann, and you play the piano beautifully, and
you saved my father's life." And on the piano in the house was
"Begin the Beguine" to round it off. So I played it again.

4

Raising Families

ALTHOUGH women's participation in American public life changed during the war years, women's roles as wives, mothers, and homemakers remained in high esteem. Of the more than 32 million married women nationwide, fewer than 10 percent had husbands absent as a result of military duty. For these women, domestic burdens grew, as they learned to do many of the tasks that men had previously performed. For all homemakers, the war made everyday responsibilities more difficult, though of course not to the extent suffered by women in war zones in Europe, Africa, and Asia. Rationing of food, clothing, and shoes and other shortages made daily tasks even more difficult as well, as did an acute shortage of housing (particularly near war-production centers) that forced many families to move in with relatives or to live with other families. In addition, to help the war effort, the government prohibited the production of many household goods after September, 1942. This caused shortages of many common household items, including can openers, toasters, towels, and knives. Ownership of appliances such as washing machines and refrigerators declined during the war. For those households with cars, gasoline and tire rationing proved a hardship.

Women coped with these difficulties as best they could. Family members pitched in, and those who did not hold outside jobs would wait in line for rationed goods for others or provide child care. Support networks evolved, particularly among pregnant women, who faced additional problems in obtaining diapers, cribs, and other baby supplies. To combat food shortages, people started victory gardens, in which they grew vegetables to supplement the rations available from stores. In short, as Jean Lechnir, Rose Truckey, and Grace Bracker illustrate, women found ways to get by.

Jean Lechnir

Jean (Hahn) Lechnir was born in 1917 in Prairie du Chien and has lived
there her entire life. She received a B.S. degree from La Crosse State
Teachers College before marrying Ray Lechnir in 1940. The Lechnirs had
two small children and Jean was pregnant with a third when her husband
was drafted for military duty in 1944 and sent to Europe, where he served
until 1945. The Lechnirs later had three more children, and when their
youngest child entered school in the early 1960's, Jean returned to work,
holding a variety of jobs until her retirement in 1978. Her husband died in
1981.

What was your wedding like?

It was the cheapest thing you could have. We got married at 7:30 in
the morning in St. John's Catholic Church. I had just a kind of suit
dress and hat — you had to wear a hat in those days. My husband
and I, well, we charged it all because we had no money. We had fifty
dollars between us. My stepmother and my dad had a breakfast for
us at their home, which was the most economical way we could
entertain the relatives after the ceremony. My uncle, who was a
wealthy man, and his wife had just bought a new coupe car. I think
it was a Buick. Anyway, they let us have that car to go to Wisconsin
Dells for our honeymoon over the weekend or three, four days, and
the whole honeymoon cost us fifty dollars. You could rent a cottage
for two dollars a night. You ran to a central bathhouse; all you did
was sleep in the cottage. So we went to the Dells and we had a ball,
but nobody had any money in those days. The war was on in Europe, a lot of men went over to England to fly for England. We had
a lot of air force fellows over there flying for England, and I think
everybody, even before the Japanese thing, were girding themselves
up for that, figuring we're going over to Germany and get rid of
Hitler or we're going to do something.

Do you think that you were financially worse off during the war?

By the time my husband went into the war, as far as I can remember, I think he was getting maybe forty, fifty dollars a week then,
and we were feeding two youngsters, and fortunately we were in this
home. After my second daughter was born we were living in a house
with a pump in the sink and an outdoor outhouse, you might say,
and I wasn't used to that. I was born and raised in a modern home
with steam heat and a bathroom. Well, I thought I was going to just
die, to take that, especially in the wintertime. So my grandparents
owned this home and they said, "You're going to move in here with
your babies and you got babies coming." (Tom was going to be

born.) "Move down there where you're going to have at least some kind of comfort." Well, then we moved in here, and it was shortly after that we found out that Ray had to go into the service. Even so, we paid Grandpa and Grandma fifteen dollars a month to live here in order to pay the taxes. . . . That was a break for us because money was short. Anyway, like I said, Ray took the only fifty dollars we had, and the government paid me eighty dollars a month. And then for each child I think I got ten dollars extra, and it was tough, real tough, but I had wonderful people over in the grocery stores that helped us out a lot.

Were you able to buy things like groceries on credit?

If you wanted to, yes, you could. The grocers were wonderful to us. I also had a victory garden, and my husband left me with a whole passel of pigeons that he was raising. So I decided I'd better kill those, that's something we could eat, because I couldn't go uptown and buy beef roast or anything like that. If we could buy hamburger, you got maybe three pounds for a dollar, something like that. I don't remember exactly the price. And if you paid your bill maybe the grocer would throw you in a ring of bologna free. Now

Jean Lechnir with her children, (l.-r.) Nancy (two years old), Tom (six months), and Pat (three years), Prairie du Chien, Easter, 1945.

Courtesy Jean Lechnir. WHi(X3)48318

bologna is more expensive than steak. . . . And, of course, butter was rationed, coffee was rationed. Everything was rationed when you come right down to it — anything that was worthwhile. Then my grandparents, they helped a lot. [My grandfather] had a big garden, too, where he sold produce, so that kept me going, and we canned everything we could get our hands on.

And then the pigeons, of course. . . . There I was, pregnant with this baby boy and I thought, "Gosh, I haven't any meat, so I'll go out and I'll kill these pigeons." I think there was maybe five or six left after my husband had left. So I got out there and I grabbed the pigeons and I had a block of wood and a hatchet and I was standing out in the back yard and I'd come up with the hatchet and I'd just get to the pigeon's neck and I couldn't do it. So my neighbor, who was also a cousin, he came over and he said, "What are you trying to do?" I said, "I'm trying to kill these pigeons because I haven't any money for meat and I've got to cook them up for the kids." The two little girls were old enough to eat something like that. He said, "Here, let me try it." He'd come up and down with the hatchet and he couldn't do it either. So finally his father come over, and he said, "What in the world is going on over here?" And he said, 'Well, we're trying to kill these pigeons. Jean wants to clean them so she can feed the kids." So he takes this hatchet and whack, whack, whack, and the pigeons were all done right like that. After that I could clean them and fix them up, but I just didn't have nerve enough to kill them. Funny — I don't know, I had nerve enough to kill squirrels and everything, but I couldn't do the pigeons. So I cleaned them up and I cooked them, and do you know, I had the worst time talking my little girls into eating them. They were pets, so — but we ate them anyway because I couldn't afford to do anything else. You ate anything that swam, crawled, or flew in order to eat cheaply.

What did you typically eat?

Hamburger. Now understand, I had these little kids so they couldn't eat steak anyway, well, I couldn't afford it, so you bought things like the hamburger, and we ate a lot of cereal. In those days cereal was cheap, very cheap. You could buy a box of cereal for fifty cents. And oatmeal — many, many night meals were just cereal.

Did your life change after your husband was called up into the service?

There was no money to do anything with. If we women got our money the first of the month, we'd get together . . . and we'd go out to eat to one of the local nightclubs or restaurants.

Without the kids, I presume?

Oh yeah. I had an aunt and they had a mother or they had a sister or somebody that would baby-sit so we didn't have to pay a baby-sitter. And then you've got to understand that maybe a top meal was $2.50. So $2.50 and maybe we could have a cocktail or a glass of pop or something for another twenty-five or fifty cents. That was our evening. But we'd extend it long enough to sit and watch other people dance or just sit and reminisce or compare notes of the letters we got from our husbands and what we thought they were doing or what we knew they were doing because all our letters were censored, of course.

Did the war cause any other problems with shortages?

Oh, definitely. I mean everything was rationed, and you had to wait in line to get butter or coffee and all us ladies that had husbands in the war — there were nine of us — we formed a card club, and that lasted for forty-eight years, our friendship. We lost some, we lost some husbands. But the main thing when we joined this club, when we played cards, the prize would be a pound of butter or a bag of sugar or a pound of coffee because we would hoard that. That's a horrible word to say — hoard. But we'd save our ration stamps and, of course, with our little babies and kids we didn't use a lot of coffee at times, not like we drink it now, and the butter was something else used very sparingly.

How often did you get together?

Every two weeks. Then we would read our husbands' letters or tell all the stuff that went on and we got very close, very close relationship with these gals. And then after our husbands got back we kept right on going with the club. I think we were closer than our husbands were, really. Of course, they had different interests in business and so forth where we women could get together and talk about children and husbands and same old thing. It's forty-eight years, I think, and I still have two of them left that are friends, but we've lost some to cancer and death and [some] moved away. But it was great. It was stability for we women because we had this thing in common and we could sympathize with each other and worry together and compare notes.

Did you provide child care for each other?

We didn't have to, because all nine of us had relatives or fathers or mothers or aunts and uncles or somebody who could step in and help. We didn't really have to baby-sit for each other, although there were groups in town that did have baby-sitting services that they would baby-sit for each other. Those were especially women that maybe were new in Prairie du Chien area or something of that sort. In fact, that's still going on with certain groups, where they, rather than send them to day care, they baby-sit for each other. But we never really had to.

What was it like to go and roll bandages?

Like a quilting bee. Yeah, everybody giggling, laughing, and we'd bring a dish to pass like they do now. Whatever you managed to get together and salvage, you put it together, and [we had] a lot of wild hot dishes in those days because if you didn't have chicken you threw in tuna fish, and if you didn't have tuna fish you threw in something else. Of course this is a great fishing country, you know, and they smoke fish and pickle fish and you do anything you can with fish around here. So there was lots of things that you could have — fish fries and those things over on the river bank.

Did you feel like you were all alone after your husband was drafted?

Yes. At first you feel abandoned and you feel angry because they took him when you needed him more at home. Then you turn around and you feel proud because he was not afraid to go. He was afraid — they were all afraid — but he went and he was doing his duty, and we figured that was part of our job is to give our husband to the war effort and to do the best we could without him. You see, the first angry feeling is we're angry at Hitler, we're angry at the Japanese, so put everything forth you could to get rid of both factions. But then after a while you have lonely times, and especially when I had my son and my husband wasn't with me, and the lady in the bed next to me or across the hall, her husband was allowed to come home to be with her with his sailor suit on, and I was alone and that was a very traumatic time.

My aunt that helped take care of the kids when I needed a baby-sitter — now, if you can picture this, this woman weighed about four hundred pounds and was six foot tall, and she was big, but she had a heart of gold. So she went to the hospital with me. Well, if you can imagine this four-hundred-pound woman pounding up and down a hall. She was one that couldn't take a lot of stress. "Oh my God, what are we going to do? Oh my God, she's in labor! Oh my God, she's in pain!" Finally, the nurse had to tell her to go sit out in the waiting room somewhere, to get out of there because she was driving everybody nuts. I wasn't having so much trouble as she was. And then it got to be kind of funny because I could just see this woman [walking] up and down the halls, just waving her arms. She never could take much. And then we got to laughing about it and then Tom's birth wasn't quite so bad. But it was the aftermath when this other gal's husband came in and mine was down in Arkansas being trained to go overseas. But it all worked out. I got a picture of [the baby] and sent it to Ray. He went out and got drunk as a lord because he had a son finally because he had all these girls.

*   *   *   *   *

Rose Truckey
Born to Armenian immigrants in 1924 in Racine, Rose (Arakelian) Truckey was originally named Nazeli, but her father changed her name to

Rose and Sy Truckey, Racine, ca. 1944.

Rose because a grade school teacher could not spell or pronounce the more traditional Armenian name. During World War II, Truckey got a job at the J. I. Case Company in Racine, working as a riveter on a production line that manufactured bomb bay doors for aircraft. While working at Case, she met Sy Truckey, who was on medical leave from the army. They married in June, 1944, and moved briefly to Rockford, Illinois. When her husband was again shipped overseas, Truckey, who had become pregnant, returned to Racine and found a job at Zahn's Department Store. Following the war, Truckey worked in a Racine bank and advanced as far as vice-president prior to her retirement in 1992. A widow since 1968, she still lives in Racine and was chosen as Ms. Senior Wisconsin in 1990. She has also served on Governor Tommy Thompson's Committee on Aging and on the Salvation Army Advisory Board, and she is a past president of the Point West Business and Professional group.

People just did not like to see a pregnant woman behind a counter. It was considered gauche, not well taken. So I think I was starting to show, I must have been about six months pregnant, and then I quit and then I stayed home. And you get a fifty-dollar-a-month allotment [from the army] to live on, which, of course, is not much because you're starting to buy all these things for the baby. You're looking for diapers, and they didn't have diapers then. You had flannel and you would wash these things. But then you couldn't even buy flannel because it was the war. Well, the man next door to us worked at Penney's. He was the assistant manager, and so when flannel came in he brought me a bolt of flannel, so we cut that up and made diapers of that. It was terrible, really, when you stop to think of it. You just couldn't get anything. I had a highchair from when I was a very little girl, a little child, so we had that. But we bought a buggy. We found one of those collapsible buggies, so we were lucky. They didn't have all the things for children that they have now, but we managed, I guess. . . .

Most of my friends were also married and/or having a child, so we kind of were our own little group. We protected one another. When one of the girls was to go have her child, she was just eighteen, and, gee, I was nineteen. Her mother had died and so a group of us took her to the hospital and she had the baby, a little boy, and I think a week later her husband was killed in action. Imagine eighteen, a new baby — those were not very nice times. I remember when Nancy [Truckey's daughter] was born on April 11, [1945,] and then on April 12, President Roosevelt died and the gal in the bed opposite me, her husband was in the navy and we were frightened. We said, "My God, now that he's dead, will our husbands come home?" You know, "What?" We were frightened. But it all worked

out, they came home. . . . You could always make sure that somebody would be there if you needed them because you couldn't depend on a man, there weren't any around. So it was really what we
could do for ourselves.

*   *   *   *   *

Grace Bracker

Grace (Peck) Bracker was born in Hazelton, Iowa, in 1911 and grew up
in numerous small Iowa towns. She received an education degree from the
University of Dubuque in 1931 and taught school in Iowa until she
married Bernhard Bracker in 1939. The couple subsequently moved to
Madison, where she worked as a part-time cook and housekeeper for her
landlord. When Bracker was pregnant with her first child, in 1942, she
and her husband moved to Edgerton, southeast of Madison, where they
remained for the duration of the war. After living in New Mexico from
April to December, 1950, the Brackers settled permanently in Madison,
where Grace taught in the public school system from 1953 until her
retirement in 1977. Her husband died in 1965.

What was life like in Edgerton?

There was a group of young women who had gotten together as a
sewing club, and eventually they were all pregnant so they decided

Courtesy Grace Bracker. WHi(X3)48296

Grace Bracker with her son, Stephen, Edgerton, ca. 1944.

to call it Baby Club. The young woman who lived up above us in our apartment [building] belonged to it, and I was obviously pregnant, and so she asked me if I wouldn't like to belong to it. It was the greatest little organization I ever belonged to. We didn't have any officers, we didn't have any dues. I suppose now you'd call it a support group. We traded off clothes, we traded off baby equipment — none of us ever bought everything. There was always somebody with a crib or a bathtub or whatever we needed. We would maybe buy one thing and then that would go the rounds when we were through with it. We would get together and knit soakers because you couldn't get rubber pants for babies. We met once a week, and if the babies had already been born we brought them along. Our babies are all grown up now and fifty years old, but every so often we get together.

Were any of these women's husbands away at war?

Yes. I was the oldest in the group and [my husband] Ben was the oldest of the men, and we lost some people because . . . they went home to live with their parents when their husbands went to war. That was, of course, always a sad time. [All of the men] came back, so we felt pretty lucky about that. Then the other thing we did was have big gardens. . . . We had no idea how much you can get out of a garden and we just didn't know what to do with it all, especially beans, I remember. That year I canned, and I canned over four hundred quarts of vegetables and fruit that year. So we didn't use very many of our ration [stamps]. . . . I don't think we ate any better and it didn't save us any money the first year, at least, because we had to buy all those fruit jars. But you use those over again. Maybe we ate better, I don't know. We just were not dependent upon the ration books. I told my son the first thing his dad did after he was born was to go out and buy me some flowers and the second thing was to go out and get [the baby's] ration book because we wanted the sugar. Otherwise, it didn't make too much difference, but the sugar was an inconvenience — not a hardship, an inconvenience.

What were the products that you grew and canned?

Beans and peas and tomatoes. We had any kind of beans that you could mention: yellow beans, lima beans, baby lima beans, green beans, pole beans. Let's see, what else did I can? Beets, carrots, corn — I canned all those, too.

A 1944 poster urging women to support rationing efforts.

Did you use all those cans during the winter?

No, we didn't, not that four hundred. We still had some left over, so the next year we didn't plant such a big garden. I planted more to flowers; it was all plowed up, [and] we needed to use it for something. We probably put our rows a little farther apart. I know I put in more flowers the next year, and I gave away as much food as I could, but almost everybody else had a garden, too. . . . We had a canning bee at the church one night and we each brought a bushel of tomatoes and some jars. I don't remember how many bushels of tomatoes we canned that night. We gave it all to the hospital, and that was one way to get rid of some of our surplus.

Did it ever strike you as ironic that you were planting flowers in your victory garden because there was too much food?

Well, yes, yes, it certainly did. And to have such an abundance of food when Europe was starving, it just really put you on a guilt trip, and you wished you could do something. We sent food boxes to Britain, as well as clothes, but of course we couldn't send fresh food or food canned in glass. We did, however, use our ration stamps for tinned food and send it over. There was extra motivation: I had relatives there.

*   *   *   *   *

World War II had a special impact on members of several groups, including Italians, Jews, and blacks. Wisconsin had small populations of all these groups at the time of World War II, and they all vigorously supported the war despite the discrimination they often suffered. Furthermore, as Anne Dinsmore explains, in addition to the hardships faced by the general population, Italian Americans feared reprisals because Italy was fighting on the Axis side. With the internment of much of the United States's Japanese population, Italians worried that they would be subject to the same treatment. Eleanor Schiff describes how American Jews felt a singular urgency about the war because of Nazi anti-Semitism. The details and extent of the Holocaust would not be known until later, but Germany had begun enacting anti-Semitic legislation before the war, and the tide of refugees that began in the 1930's attested to the poor conditions for Jews under Nazi domination. Finally, Rubie Bond expresses the black community's perspective on the war and describes her contributions to the war effort.

Anne Dinsmore

Born in Madison in 1916 to Sicilian immigrants, Anne (Aparatore) Dinsmore was graduated from the University of Wisconsin in 1938 with a degree in social work. She worked for several years with the Girl Scouts of America in Omaha, Nebraska, but at the start of World War II, she returned to Madison to be with her family. She married in 1943 and gave birth to a son in 1944, after her husband left to serve in the war. They later divorced, and in 1966 she joined the Peace Corps, spending two years in South America. After she returned to the United States, Anne remarried and lived for the next several years in the Middle East, primarily in Saudi Arabia. She is divorced and still lives in Madison.

So I was at home with a child, and my job primarily was to read the letters that all the sons wrote home, to write letters, and to interpret the news, what was happening. When [the older people in the community] couldn't read it in English and it wasn't coming to [them] in Italian, I'm sure it was frightening. And so I would explain [the news]. . . . Now, many of our brothers, sons, were everywhere, scattered all over the world. [People would ask,] "Where is New Guinea? What is it? Who lives there?" You see, you had to do geography lessons. "I know where Italy is, but where is England?" "It's over here; see this map."

Courtesy Anne Dinsmore. WHi(X3)48335
Anne Dinsmore with her son, Phillip Shallat, Madison, 1949.

We put up a map. It was almost like a command post, just to try to explain where their children were, where our brothers were. And that was a very poignant time. The women had some fears that after the Japanese were rounded up and sent to internment camps, they began to fear — when Italy was still on the side of the Axis, the German Axis — they began to fear that if things got really tough in Italy, [if people] persisted in supporting Hitler, their lives would be pretty miserable here, and maybe we'd all be interned for one reason or another. And I kept saying, "No, that can't be. You see, your sons, our brothers, are fighting in this war." Well, of course, so were the Japanese. And they said, "Yeah, but aren't the Japanese fighting, too?" "Yes, they are." "Why should we be exempt? What are they going to do with the Germans?" So, you see, that was the big fear. It didn't happen. Italy changed its allegiance to the Allies [in 1943], and then we knew it couldn't happen. We hoped it wouldn't happen.

But those were very, very anxious times, very anxious times. Nobody knew who was coming back, if anything, and, of course, any news that brought the death of any one of our friends, any one of the young men of the neighborhood, was a tragedy for all people, everyone. . . .

And the mothers, our mothers, were very busy at the local settlement house wrapping bandages like crazy, making Red Cross kits, and knitting. We were all knitting at home. Knitting and sewing and heaven knows what, and there was a very faithful core of neighborhood women who supplied the Red Cross with everything that they asked for.

When you returned during the war, did you see a difference in the way that Italians were viewed in Madison?

The difference lay in the fact that all the young men were gone, or the ones of fighting age were gone. They were not there. The community was held together by women. Women are pretty strong and our mothers were like the Rock of Gibraltar. They had always coped. Italian women had always coped. They had the nitty-gritty of family problems. Men always tended to shy away. The men — in the context of World War II, we're talking about the young men of fighting age — but their fathers fell apart when they saw them going off to war. Just fell apart. And it was the women who stood very strong and kept families together, kept families together.

The men during that time, because there was an Italian Workingman's Club — that's still there over on Regent Street — which was a really safe haven for the men, which is where they played cards and garbled their syntax and tried to talk about world affairs, and only those walls know how they presented these problems. It was hysterical. . . . They were illiterate in their own language, and it was only a few of them who could read in Italian, and there were newspapers published in Italian — but [they were] published in the East, in Boston, in New York — which gave the news. And the men who could read — and there were some — would take their newspapers over to the club and give them all the news. Or, if they held still, their daughters read the news in English and then told them what it was all about. But, yes, the [Italian] community — that was probably the beginning of the end, the Second World War. It cracked that community wide open. We began to have things in common with the community at large, which is, "Your sons are going to war; well, so are mine." And there began to be a feeling of oneness with a larger community.

The Red Cross was delighted with the Italian women because, by God, they were faithful, loyal, industrious, trying to outdo every other women's group in the city. Turning out more bandages, more this, more that, knitting more things, sewing more things, and they thought, "By God, we'll show them that the Italian ladies can do this, too." Well, they did themselves quite proud there.

Yes, it was inevitable that the world stage at that time, which was World War II, was also the beginning of the end for completely tight ingrained community. The mores couldn't hold. You couldn't hold your girls back like you were doing before. Some of them had to get jobs away from the community, away from the particular neighborhood. You let your girls stay in high school longer, because many of our friends didn't graduate. They dropped out to get married. Many of the girls graduated from high school after that and did very well, too. The young men, when they returned, couldn't be held still much longer either. Although they were always free to come and go, they felt a certain loyalty to staying where they were. Well, some went to school under the GI Bill, which was wonderful; some with their mustering-out pay. Of course, many married, began to move away from the neighborhood.

There were at one time definite legal or tacit restrictions to buying property outside of the Italian community. Italians were not welcome, absolutely not welcome. Found that out when . . . [a family that] had five sons — all of them were educated — they actually went to buy a house and were told, "Oh, yeah?" Even though they had the money to put down, they were refused. Later on, years later, they did buy a house outside the community, but after that time, after a certain amount of time, there weren't any restrictions.

*   *   *   *   *

Eleanor Schiff

> Born in 1914 in Lorain, Ohio, to Jewish immigrants from eastern Europe, Eleanor (Shiff) Schiff was graduated from Ohio State University in 1938. She married Philip Schiff later that year, and the couple moved to Clarksburg, West Virginia, in January, 1939. They had a son in 1940, a daughter in 1943, and another son seven years later. Shortly after the attack on Pearl Harbor, the Schiffs moved to the Milwaukee suburb of Shorewood, where Eleanor continues to reside. Following her husband's death in 1963, Eleanor opened a travel agency, which she ran until 1988. She remains active in a number of civic and charitable causes.

Did you find the Jewish community to be particularly cohesive during the war?

I think so. I think everybody felt a common bond, a little bit more than maybe normal, because everybody worried about everyone else. Everyone had somebody in the service and there was a constant worry.

Did you have any idea of the atrocities that were occurring in Germany?

Yes, as [refugees] began to come out, we did know, we did know. And, of course, they tried to send money and they tried to do things for people and they tried to get people out, but the situation was not a good one. And we couldn't understand how Hitler could just walk through the whole world. And everything you read was very slow in getting [to the United States] and people were slow in reacting, I think, too, as we look back at all the atrocities. . . . Our rabbi preached [about the atrocities] . . . and so we were very much aware of it, and we read. There didn't seem to be a lot that we could do. We were, at that point, contributing. They were trying to get people out to go to [Palestine] and there were people that were helping take care of Jews that were in hiding, and so we tried to support them with financial amounts to help. It was a very, very, very frightening time, and we as citizens could only do what we were asked to do and that was to contribute because the heads of the countries weren't able to stem all this fighting.

Did it seem to you that the country as a whole was doing enough for the European Jews?

We didn't think so, we didn't think so. But of course a war was going on. You just never know. It was just so unreal and so horrendous that it was hard to believe that somebody couldn't do something about it, and they obviously couldn't, because they didn't. And they say [the American government] didn't know, but I think there was enough evidence to show that they did know. And some of it of course wasn't believable, that one man [Hitler] can just step forward and have such destruction.

What sort of things did the Jewish community or the synagogue organize in terms of aiding the war effort?

They did everything in their power to get people out of there and some came here, some went to [Palestine], some went to South America. Oh, and they had the bond drives and they had the stuff where they sent food to people and they sent clothing to people. They were a cohesive group that did try to make a difference, and I'm sure in some instances they did. But there wasn't a lot you could do. When there's a war and all these atrocities are happening, the hands over here aren't going to help what's going on there, and the governments couldn't even stop it, you know — Paris, France, England, Czechoslovakia, any of them. [The Germans] just marched through and nobody could stop them. So the communities that weren't there, they couldn't stop any of that, they could just try to help alleviate some of the destitute people and try to get them out of there, which at that point wasn't happening that fast. But there are the Holocaust survivors and so somewhere along the line somebody was doing something. The atrocities, it was hard to imagine, to believe, and you were stunned to hear some of the things when everything finally came out.

Was there a different sort of community of women during the war?

Yes, there was, and I remember to this day this one gal always says she thinks we were so wonderful because we always made it our business to have somebody over for dinner or if we were going to a movie to call somebody up to see if they wouldn't like to go with us, because they were alone and they were alone with their children. So we did try very, very hard to include people who weren't as fortunate as we were.

So I remember this one gal who subsequently got married and . . . she kept saying to her husband, "They were so good to me. You should have seen when you were in the service, they took me to dinner and [included me in other social events]." Well, it meant something to people and for us it was just a natural thing to do. But we were very careful to include a lot of people in everything we did, one at a time or two at a time or a family. If we went on an outing over at Hubbard Park or anything and then we used to cook outside, we always made it our business to include someone less fortunate than we were. We were very fortunate. We were the kind of family that always lived by counting our blessings.

*   *   *   *   *

Rubie Bond

Rubie (White) Bond was born in Pontotoc, Mississippi, in 1906 and remained there until the First World War, when her parents, seeking economic opportunities unavailable to blacks in the South, moved their family to Beloit. Bond attended Beloit College, noted for its willingness to accept black students. In 1928 she married Franklin M. Bond and became a mother to his three daughters from a previous marriage. The Bonds subsequently had six additional children, five of whom were born before World War II started. Her husband died in 1985, and she still resides in Beloit.

How could you have expressed your strong feelings about civil rights during the war?

I was never much for demonstrations or anything like that, but I remember when I went to the first PTA meeting over here at Merrill School. [It was] 1940, when my children started school there. They had black children in school, but the blacks never went to the PTA meetings. But I went, and I participated in them. I would ask questions and would volunteer. And finally that sort of broke down that wall. And then we organized — this was shortly after the war was over — the women's community club here. And we invited all of the heads of all the different departments in the city to speak to us. Some of them replied and others didn't. But that's how we got the movement started to get black teachers and that sort of thing.

I remember the superintendent of schools — I went to see him about schoolteachers and that sort of thing and he said, "Well, you don't have any blacks that are intelligent enough." And I said, "Well, you just look around. You might find some." And he went away to Boston because he heard that they had an integrated school there with blacks and whites, and then he came back and he told me that he never knew that there were such intelligent blacks. And I said, "Where have you been all my life?" So, you know, we started him to thinking and we helped to educate him.

What sort of work did you do with the Red Cross?

We had a home nursing class, that you could help people who needed assistance in the home and taking care of the ill and that sort of thing because of a shortage of doctors and that sort of thing. My physician that we'd had for something like forty years, when my youngest son was born [in 1946], I had to get another doctor for him because [his doctor] had gone into the navy.

Did everyone buy war bonds?

I don't think everyone had to, but, my husband signed up for a payroll deduction and [would] buy bonds through that. And then we would get so much in savings and I would buy a bond. I remember going to this meeting for the Girl Scouts and telling this gal I'd just come from the bank to buy a bond during the war, to support the war, so she could sit behind her mahogany, polished desk and tell me that black girls couldn't be in the Girl Scout troops in the schools. And I wore one winter coat for sixteen years, and I had war bonds, had bonds, and had money in the bank. I could have bought a coat, but I used that money to support the war.

5

Being Young and in School

ALMOST 10 percent of Wisconsin's women over age fourteen were in school during the war years, most of them in high school. Too young to hold full-time jobs and generally with fewer family responsibilities, this group concentrated on schoolwork, helping around the house, and war-related volunteer work. Marjorie Miley, Gene Gutkowski, and Annastasia Batikis were all between the ages of fourteen and sixteen when the war began, and they grew to maturity during an era of uncertainty and upheaval. Their descriptions of the war's effect on their lives offer a different perspective from that of older women and include their outlooks on ethnicity, dating, and changes in their daily lives.

Marjorie Miley

Although born in Sheboygan in 1925, Marjorie Miley has lived most of her life in Manitowoc, on the Lake Michigan shore. After graduating from high school in 1943, she took a job as a proofreader at the Manitowoc *Herald Times* (later the *Herald Times Reporter*). She spent her entire career with the newspaper, eventually rising to become its managing editor, the first and only woman to serve in that post. During World War II, Manitowoc became a center for the shipbuilding industry, including the Manitowoc Shipbuilding Company, which built submarines, and the Burger Boat Company, which manufactured landing vehicles. Mirro Aluminum also did a considerable amount of defense manufacturing. This situation created a large influx of people to Manitowoc and dramatically altered the nature of this lakeside community.

What are some of the first things that you remember changing as a result of the start of the war?

I think the thing that affected us most, as students, was that the senior boys in the class ahead of us were already enlisting and leaving and by the time we graduated in 1943, between forty-five and fifty of the boys weren't in high school anymore. They received their diplomas either by mail or their mothers came and got them for them. But out of our class of 430 kids there were forty-five already in the service by the time we graduated. . . .

A lot of us — not me, but a lot of the kids, especially those taking commercial courses — had jobs down at the shipyard. They would leave school early in the afternoon and go down to the yards and work in the office — those were the girls. And the boys, some of them had factory jobs at the shipyards. I know there was this picture in our high school annual of the lunch bucket brigade from Lincoln High School going to work at the shipyards.

I happened to work at a local theater, the Strand Theater. . . . A good many of our customers were the sailors who were here for the training for the submarine program because they did their training aboard the ships in Manitowoc, and there was a big barracks here for the single sailors. I think every apartment in Manitowoc or anything that could be made into an apartment was rented by the married ones.

It made quite a difference in the social life of people my age. There weren't too many fellows around to go out with, they were all going off into the service, and quite a few girls — four or five or six

Courtesy Loa Fergot. WHi(X3)48524

Myrtle Koch, Doris Kuchenbecker, Janet Arndt, Shirley Christopher, Mary Jane Uvaas, Loa Fergot, and Lillian Hildebrand around the time of their graduation from Neenah High School, June, 1942.

in our class — married submarine sailors. . . . [The war] made a big difference in the social life in Manitowoc. There was, of course, the social life of the officers of the submarines, which was different than the social life of the enlisted people. Most of the officers were married and they brought their wives here and sometimes their families if they were here for a while, but the enlisted men, for the most part, were very young and were not married, so this town was pretty lively during those years. Some of the bars downtown were special hangouts for the sailors and with all the people working at the shipyards, the entire social structure of the city changed there for about four or five years while all of this was going on.

The shipyards itself had 7,000 people working there, so there were a lot of new families that came into town. And working at the theater, we noticed how much business we got from the submarine sailors. They liked to come there. The admission price in those days was forty-four cents, and they could come and bring their girlfriends and get in for eighty-eight cents and still have some money left over to spend later for popcorn. They were good customers.

Then the other thing that we noticed in high school was when the rationing started — the issuance of rationing books for canned goods and sugar and eventually meat and gasoline, coffee, and shoes. The superintendent of schools in Manitowoc was the overall chairman for rationing and those of us who were seniors at Lincoln went out to the various places where rationing books were issued and we were the issuing agents of the ration books. People were supposed to declare how much canned goods they had at home and how much sugar and then we were supposed to rip out the corresponding number of stamps from the ration book. Of course, we never did know if people were really declaring what they had at home or not. But we were trained and we did this for the spring semester for one social studies class and it was interesting. It was a different thing to do. I still have some ration books that our family had.

Of course, I wasn't doing the cooking then, my mother was, and it never bothered me, any of the shortages. I'm sure she was bothered. I don't recall that we ever went without a whole lot. I mean it's just that sometimes when you wanted coffee or chocolate or sugar or meat, it just wasn't available, and you had to go back when it was available. It was an interesting time. I imagine if my mother was still living she could be more specific about things she went without. I know some of my friends who were married during that time had to give their ration books to the bakeries making their wedding cakes

*Marjorie Miley,
Manitowoc, 1943.*

Courtesy Marjorie Miley. WHi(X3)48263

so that they would have enough sugar. They had to give them sugar stamps so they'd have enough sugar to make their wedding cakes, especially if they wanted frosting on them. These are just some of the little things.

Do you think that Manitowoc during this period could be called a boom town?

Oh yes, oh yes. Quite a few of the other factories besides the ship-building company were completely involved in World War II, like the Mirro Aluminum Company. They were making canteens and shell boxes and some other things. I think their entire production was into war production and they had guards at all their doors to make sure that unauthorized people didn't get in. They also had guards at the shipyards. There's a vantage point here in town where you can look down on the shipyards from a park down to the river and to the shipyards, and they used to scan that all the time to make sure people weren't taking pictures from up there of the submarines under construction. I don't know how they could possibly have caught everybody who might have pointed a camera that way. I had a front seat on all the war news because after I graduated from high school I went to work at the newspaper and we got all the war news, of course, over the Associated Press, and the local news of what had happened to the local servicemen. I was always up to date on what was going on.

*   *   *   *   *

Gene Gutkowski

Eugenia ("Gene") (Amrhein) Gutkowski was born in Milwaukee in 1927 to Catholics of German descent. She left high school in 1943 to help her family financially when her brother left for military service, working at Steinmeyer's Grocery Store until the late 1940's. She then worked at Sealtest Dairy until her marriage to Alfred Gutkowski in 1953. Since that time she has been a homemaker, and she still lives in Milwaukee with her husband.

Was your neighborhood mostly German, or were there a lot of different ethnicities?

We were strictly German. Even our church had words in German written in it. Our neighboring area was upper Polish. There was the upper Polish, which was supposed to be the higher class, the upper is. The lower was on the south side, and in those days [most people] did not intermix. The Germans stuck together and the Polish, etc. So my sister had gotten married to this very fine young Polish man the month before, at Thanksgiving [1941], right before the war started. So my dad was really upset that she married a Polish person, because my father was pro-German. All his relatives were in Germany. His father came over, and some of his brothers were even born over there. So when the war started after a while with Germany, then my father — he just didn't think it was right for us to be fighting the Germans. And the teenagers, being what teenagers are, we weren't afraid to stand up to my father and we were trying to explain to him that there are Germans, and there are Germans. They were not all Nazis, and some did not like it any more than the rest of us. But it took him a long time. He was praying that our brother, his son, would not have to go and fight his own relatives. So I'm thankful my brother was sent to Japan and New Guinea. But oh, yes, the Polish people didn't like the Germans.

How did they express their dislike of the Germans in your neighborhood?

They didn't want you to date. And if you'd go out with someone that was a different nationality, and the other people would make it

*Gene Gutkowski,
Milwaukee, 1944.*

Courtesy Gene Gutkowski; WHi(X3)48329

well known that you were not accepted. "You are German and your people are hurting ours — like the Polish." I married a Polish man, and I love him, and we've been married for going on thirty-nine years. In fact, I married a Polish [man] from the south side — the lower class. But [when I was growing up] we lived always on the north side. And my whole family lives on the north side — excepting me. But through the years, then, my father got to understand finally that we were right. All the Germans weren't Nazis — that it was Hitler and his followers, and some of the poor young men who were German had to fight, even if they didn't believe in him. And it was the same with the Italians. People were against the Italians because of Mussolini, who was with Hitler. It was real tough dating because you had to really pick out who you were going to go out with.

Were you dating a German boy when the war broke out?

Oh, yes. He lived around the corner by us, and he was my brother's boyfriend, and that's how I met him. I was very young, in those days I was young. I was thirteen. We could not go out alone. My father would not allow that. He was very strict. I could go out if I double-dated with my brother — if he had a girlfriend or if he came along. But I could not go out with [my boyfriend] alone. And in fact, no cars — we had to take the streetcars. We had to take those if we had to go anywhere.

Did your brother date mostly German girls?

German, Irish. During the war? Well, I only had my brother Connie, who was the one in the navy, was going out with an Irish girl.

How did your father react to that?

That was okay. Irish were fine.

Interesting.

Yes, it was. There was a Jew that was across the street from us that we weren't even allowed to play with, which I think is wrong — I think it's very wrong. But that's the way it was in those days. You had your own little cliques. That's the way it was.

Were there a lot of people in your neighborhood who had relatives in Germany?

Oh, I would think so, yes. In fact, my boyfriend's parents had relatives. And what hurt my father, too, was because his father was in the service, in the German army. He fought under the Kaisers. And so it really hurt my father that this was his land. And he just couldn't see anything wrong there. We did not get much news, and when you did it was all from the one side — our side. You never saw the other side. It was so much propaganda. And, let's face it, we were very patriotic. The United States could do nothing wrong in those days.

*   *   *   *   *

Annastasia Batikis

Born in 1927 in Kaukauna, Annastasia Batikis was youngest of three children of Greek immigrants from Constantinople. Her parents, who moved the family to Racine in 1929, spoke little English and emphasized Greek customs in the home. Batikis's mother died during World War II, leaving her with responsibility for caring for the household. Throughout her childhood, Batikis had a strong interest in athletics, and in the spring of 1945 she tried out for the All-American Girls' Professional Baseball League and won a position on the Racine Belles, playing for one season. She worked as a secretary in the Racine school system from 1945 until 1948, when she enrolled at La Crosse State Teachers College, receiving a B.S. in 1952 and a master's degree in 1960. She taught in the Manitowoc schools from 1952 to 1954 and in the Racine public schools from 1954 until her retirement in 1985. She still lives in Racine with her brother, John.

My dad worked at J. I. Case Company and the three of us were still in school. My brothers graduated from high school in '41 and '42 and then shortly after that went into service, one into the air force and one into the navy. The one that went into the navy went to Pearl Harbor and then went off into different directions from there but was stationed at Pearl Harbor. John, the air force brother, was trained for a while here and then he ended up in the China-Burma-India part of the war. Of course, I was still in school, but I remember selling stamps. We sold stamps in our homerooms at school and then eventually when you filled up a book of stamps then you got a bond. I was one of the people both in junior high and in high school that was in charge of collecting the money and making sure that people got their stamps and things got taken to the office. On the home front we did things like hanging flags in our windows for the men that we had in service. I rolled bandages, we did some things for the USO. Great Lakes [Naval Training Station, in Waukegan, Illinois,] was close by, so Racine was a pretty good town for the sailors on the weekend, so we had things going for them. The church [members] invited them into their homes on Sundays so that they could have home-cooked meals. There were USO dances down at our Memorial Hall. We collected scrap iron and things like that. Of course, then rationing came, and we didn't have a car, so the gas thing didn't make any difference to us, but the sugar rationing and the meat rationing really hit kind of hard.

What were some of the first changes in your life after the war started?

Probably the rationing, and it kind of always amazed me to see so many young men on the weekends coming through. Back in those days we had what we called an interurban, and it was kind of a rapid transit thing that ran between Racine, Kenosha, and Milwaukee. They ran far enough so that the guys from Great Lakes could get on and either stop at Kenosha or Racine or go on to Milwaukee, and so all of the cities on weekends were really filled with sailors and soldiers at one point or another. Fort Sheridan [Illinois] wasn't that far beyond Great Lakes so we got [men from] both. Well, food, too, I guess that was another thing that really made a difference. I think most of us in our family had a sweet tooth, and that not being able to have sugar was really something. And then of course I noticed — and I think everybody did — that when the rationing started then

WHi(X3)48548

Governor Julius P. Heil presents an award to the winner of the
children's scrap-metal drive, May, 1942.

there was hoarding of foods too. It seemed like most people had a
little cupboard someplace that they were keeping things — storing
things.

What sort of products would get hoarded?

I can remember the sugar. I guess maybe that was the thing that I
noticed the most. I think I can remember my mom trading some of
our gas stamps or cigarette stamps for their sugar stamps and
maybe once in a while meat. But where we were, I think everybody
had enough kids that they needed all their own meat stamps. And
then the other thing was [that] the storekeepers were really good
about running up a bill for people. In some cases, some people just
didn't have the money to pay for things, and so they ran up a bill.
And as long as you paid a little bit at it, so that you weren't just
freeloading, they gave you credit, and that was something that I
remember. . . .

At school things went on as usual except that we did get involved
with the stamps and the bonds and doing things for the USO, and
the kids helped at the Red Cross and the letter writing. Some of the
club activities took on a very patriotic tinge. Everything was very

patriotic back then. Everybody was really behind everybody. Neighborhoods became, I think, very close.

In addition to the hoarding, did you ever encounter the black market?

I can remember one of our neighbors having a little space like under their steps — they had stairs going up to their second floor and then there was like a little closet underneath those steps — I can remember seeing packages of brown sugar and powdered sugar and five-pound bags of regular sugar in there. I'm sure that they had somehow — I don't know how they got it — but I'm sure it wasn't just with the stamps that we had gotten each week for things like that. As I said, we didn't have a car, so most of the time our gas stamps went to other people, but I know that two doors down that man never seemed to run out of gas, so he must have been getting some somewhere, too. But otherwise I think I probably was maybe a little bit too young to really know if they were doing really, really bad things. Our neighborhood was pretty much all working-class people, so I think they just wanted to make sure their families got fed and kept intact.

Annastasia Batikis (right) and Florence Caynale at the post office mailing letters to servicemen, Racine, winter, 1944.

Courtesy Annastasia Batikis, WHi(X3)48504

How valuable a commodity were your gasoline stamps?

I don't think they always went to the same person, but there was always a trade that went on. I don't think my parents had to go out and say, "Who wants this?" Somebody knew that we didn't have a car, so they said, "Well, can we have your gas stamps this week? We'll give you whatever." Most of the time I think it was for sugar.

What was the ethnic character of your community and your neighborhood?

On one side of us we had a Jewish family and there were Germans upstairs from them. On the other side, let's see, I think Grabers must have been part German also. We had some Finns down further and up the other way there were two Italian families and there was a black family across the street. There were Polish people on another corner and everybody had at least two or three kids. There must have been forty kids in the neighborhood just going one square block around. And if you went two or three blocks in the other direction, you probably had the same thing.

We were Greek, there was a Hungarian family and Italian. Just about everything you can think of — Polish — and we all traded things and we all exchanged, eating together at different times and picnics. I think that's where I learned to appreciate Hungarian food especially and the goodies that they make and some of the Polish things. The Italian stuff, too, but I guess I'm kind of partial to the Hungarian food. . . . Racine is known for its Danish community, so a little further down toward the lake from here it was called the "Kringleville," which was just filled with Danish people, and I went to school with them. The school that I went to was — there, too, we had just about every kind of ethnic group and the whole gamut as far as the whole economic scale is concerned too. I feel fortunate having grown up in a situation like that. . . . Even though it wasn't what today would be called an inner-city school, we all went to the same school, whether your dad worked in a factory or was a doctor or a lawyer or whatever. It was the same community school, so that was kind of neat.

Did people in the neighborhood help each other with child care?

Well, most of the mothers in our neighborhood didn't work — they stayed home and took care of their kids. In fact, I can't remember any [women] that worked, not in our block anyway. . . . If [my parents] went somewhere, the boys were old enough to [stay] by themselves or went over to play with other boys, but I went along. So there weren't any baby-sitters. The parents took their younger ones along and then you sat down and you were seen and not heard.

Did high school girls commonly go down to the USO?

Yeah, certain groups of them, anyway. Girls were still kind of under their moms' thumbs back then, so you didn't have the kind of freedom that the girls, well, that any kid has today. Again, they felt that they were doing something, they were helping [with the war effort]. We had people come over for dinner and I went to a couple of the USO dances, but more than that I was always either making cookies or writing letters or doing that kind of stuff.

What would it be like when you would have people over for dinner? Were they people you already knew?

No. Sometimes it was just some of the young men that would happen to have come to church, and you just invited them to come home with you. Sunday was chicken day at our house. That was kind of fun too because, again, for a while, anyway, it was still legal to have live chickens in the city. So my dad would go get the chicken Saturday and it would be in the basement and it would get killed on Saturday night and I ended up plucking it. Then we had fresh chicken stuff on Sunday then for dinner — soup and other things.

What role did religion play for you during the war?

It was important. So much so that I think I still have the pin. I have a pin for at least ten or twelve years of perfect attendance. Because my mother died when I was still so very young, I leaned pretty heavily on my church background and the faith that I had and the friends that I had in the church. I can still count on some of those same people.

Did the churches that you attended sponsor groups dealing directly with the war, like Red Cross or donor organizations or clothing or scrap-metal drives?

Well, I think everybody that had somebody in the service from church did it one way or another. There was a lot of knitting going on, too. I didn't know how to knit so I didn't do that, but there was knitting, and then of course a lot of the women that would be my mom's age, they rolled bandages — did things with old sheets and stuff that they had. Some of them drove the Red Cross wagons around. And then again, when the servicemen came into town, there was always coffee and doughnuts for them. More than anything else I think it was just the idea of sharing your home with some kid that was away from home, so whenever the kids would come to church that were around the area that were in service or if one of the sons brought somebody home with them, why, they were always welcomed. Somehow they were taken in by the church family.

How did you feel about the war from the information in newsreels or on the radio? Did you always feel that the Allies would win?

I don't know whether it was just from that or whether I had just made up my mind or what, but I think all the way through the thing I felt that we were doing something that was right, and back in those days everything was either black or white to me. There weren't any shades of gray in between, so because we were doing something right, the right would win, and that was all there was to it. Since then, I think we've found out that there are other shades and degrees of things.

6

Loved Ones in Danger

NEARLY 325,000 men from Wisconsin served in some branch of
the military during World War II. Each of them left behind women — mothers, sisters, wives, and friends — who cared for them
and worried about their safety. These women followed the war av-
idly in newspapers and magazines, on the radio, and in movie newsreels, although censorship often limited the information available.
Mail from loved ones became a prized commodity, with friends and
neighbors sharing whatever information they had. On some occa-
sions, however, the news was bad. Almost 8,000 men from Wisconsin were killed during the war, and another 13,600 were wounded.

Gene Gutkowski, Rose Kaminski, Jean Lechnir, and Loa Fergot
all experienced firsthand what it was like to have someone you
loved far away and in danger. Both Gutkowski's brother and boyfriend served; Kaminski's husband served in the navy in
1944–1945; Lechnir's husband served with the army during the
same time; and Fergot's husband was a navigator in the U.S. Army
Air Corps until he was shot down and taken prisoner by the
Germans in the fall of 1944.

Gene Gutkowski

[The war] didn't really hit home when I was just in high school. It
took a long time. Because it was so far away. I mean, you thought it
would never hit us home here. Until my brother went. Then my
boyfriend went and it hit home. I cried a lot. I was very close to my
brother because he was just a little older than me. And he used to
take me out a lot. Before I had a boyfriend, he used to treat me a lot.
He was very good to me. I was worried that something might happen, and every night after work, I'd come home, drop in by church
before I'd come home, say a prayer for everybody, because the
neighbor boy went, the young man next door went, and on the

112

other side that neighbor went. Our neighbors were worried because they weren't that old — they were maybe nineteen. Now when I think about it, they seem like kids. I see my grandson now that age. It hurts you to think that these boys are going, and you don't know how they're going to come back, if they're going to come back.

I think maybe the girls who didn't have boyfriends or who were going out with a lot of fellas, maybe they felt different about it than I did. Because, see, I had the one [boyfriend], and I knew I was going to be true to him. Even when there were dances, I'd say "No thanks. I've got a boyfriend." Fellas would ask me to go out, and I'd say "No, thank you. I have a boyfriend in service." So I didn't go to anything at school, not to the prom, not to anything because I was being true. But that's me, I don't know what other girls could do. . . .

We were so glad to see my brother when he finally got here [when the war ended]. And I was glad to see my boyfriend, even though he changed. They changed so much. They went through so much. They got so serious. . . . They were not the same as they left. And up to this day, my brother speaks very little about what he saw over there. [He] saw the headhunters over there, in New Guinea. He went through a lot.

*   *   *   *   *

Rose Kaminski

Well, when the time came, my husband went. We had one child, my oldest daughter, at that time when he was called to war, and she was about three years old. My brother had already registered for service. My two brother-in-laws were in the service, so it was starting to hit us a little bit more, and we were beginning to think in terms of how it was going to affect us. My husband went to Great Lakes [Naval Training Station, in Waukegan, Illinois,] for boot camp along with hundreds of other young fellows. When we went down to Great Lakes for the final ceremony when the fellows were ranked, it was exciting. Everybody was there. All the young fellows were in uniform. We were young. That was exciting. We didn't have many exciting things in our life at that time. . . .

The fellows were sent out from boot camp to various places. I know my brother was in a submarine. My brother-in-laws were sent out to Guadalcanal. Those were bad times. We were all biting our fingernails. My husband was sent out to Norfolk, Virginia. He was put in with a unit where they did minesweeping, and to us that was danger, danger, danger. . . . We did a lot of letter writing, and we did a lot of baking and sending out packages to all the boys — my brother, my brother-in-laws, and my husband.

How often did you write? Did this form a big part of your relationship?

Oh yes, it was a big part. It was on a regular basis. I would say I'd write two times a week, three times. The fellows didn't always get the mail as regular as they would have liked to. A lot of times you'd get a letter and [it would] say, "I haven't heard from you for quite a while. How come?" Then all of sudden all the mail would come through at one time. Then there was another little gimmick that they had going downtown. They had a little store where you could go into a little booth and make records. I would take my daughter down there and we would make records, and they were little plastic records. And you would make a record and you'd tell your daughter to say hi to Daddy and then sing a song for him or something. We'd make little tapes and they would get them and they would play them. And they would play them over and over. They really liked that part of it. . . .

My husband was wounded during the service, [although] not in actual combat. He was in a minesweeper unit and they were supposed to go overseas, and they were having a practice time before they went, and when they were practicing shooting — naturally they were shooting with blanks — but they had to simulate the actual war shooting, and one of the fellows was supposed to be wounded and had fallen, and my husband was supposed to go run and help him. In the meantime, one of the shells exploded in a gun and the magazine exploded and shrapnel flew out. So he got hit with a piece of shrapnel. This was just before he went overseas. He was taken to a hospital in St. Albans, right out of New York. It was in the morning, [and] I was supposed to go pick up my daughter, and the little Western Union telegram came with the little guy on the bike. You didn't have a phone, you didn't have anybody call, so they delivered and gave me this letter. I knew right away that it had to be something, because we just never got telegrams. So I sat down on the stoop next to the porch there, and I opened up and I read it, and it [said] my husband was wounded and he was on the critical list.

I didn't know what to do. We were not used to traveling. We never flew in an airplane — though I'd been on trains, but [only] with my mother when we were kids when we traveled. I had never

A poster distributed by the War Department around 1945 urging women to write to their loved ones overseas.

been on a train alone. I didn't know where to go, who to turn to. So, I went and told his mother — because she lived about three blocks away from where I lived — about it. We called the Red Cross, because I didn't know how to get a ticket to go on a train. I didn't know where I was going to stay if I got there. I had no idea of how to handle a situation. I was young, I was inexperienced. We just never had to deal with those problems.

So the Red Cross said that they would get the ticket for me and make arrangements for me to stay at a home near the hospital. My sister-in-law . . . said she would go with me. But we would have to reimburse the Red Cross for the expenses, which was all right because we did not have the cash right on hand either. In today's dollars, it was not a huge amount, [but] at that time it seemed like quite a bit. We went and we got the train and we were headed for New York, and that was an experience. We saw more servicemen on the train, and people jammed in the train traveling. It was so different from the way we traveled when we were youngsters. My mother would go to Grandma's up in Michigan, we'd go on the train and it was a fun thing. We used to run around in the train. You saw both sides of the picture — you saw the young people happy and singing and having a good time and others sitting and downhearted and confused like I was. It was quite an experience.

When we got to New York — and we changed trains once or twice, I'm not sure anymore — but we got there eventually. We took a cab to this home that we were going to stay at. We had a very lovely room. The family opened their home to us, and it was very nice. We came during the wee hours of the morning and it was walking distance to the hospital, and someone from the family took us down to show us where we had to go. The hospitals were barracks, really, that were built off the ground. Maybe there was about a foot off the ground like the old temporary barracks were. We were taken into this office where a young lady was sitting and she took all the pertinent information that we had. I recall my sister-in-law and I were sitting there — and I'll never forget this, and it seems kind of funny, but looking down on the floor we saw this nice big cockroach, and we thought, "Oh my God, what kind of a place is this?" When you looked at the floors, you could have eaten off the floors they were so clean. We did not realize, at the time, that being so close to the ground and the dampness and everything that they had a problem. We were petrified. We just didn't know what to do. So this young lady told us, "Oh, don't worry. It's just something we learn how to cope with." When I talked to my husband later on I found out how they coped with it. But anyways, we were taken to his room and everything was just, just spotless. It was about three or four days before he was off the critical list, and we could come and go as we wanted. We could be with him all day and until he was off the critical list, and then we had to go home. I had a job to go to. . . .

So the last day — we were going home — we decided that [because] we were in New York we had to see New York. So we decided we would take one day off and go into the city and see New York, so we did. . . . We went into New York and we walked down 42nd Street, and we just gawked like hicks. It was really funny. Well, we had never seen a town that huge, and we were going to shop. Oh, we were going to be so elegant. We were going to buy something and bring it home from New York. So we went shopping, and we each bought a dress in New York, and we thought that we could go home and say this was a New York creation. And wouldn't you know, maybe about three or four months later, we saw the same dresses at Brandt's, which was quite a nice dress store in our era. That took all the air out of our sails. So, New York was not any different than Milwaukee as far as garments were considered. Right at the time we really thought we were elegant.

Like all tourists, we stopped and had our pictures taken and went from store to store, shop to shop. We went to Radio City, and we got tickets for a radio program. We explained to them that we were just in town for the one day, that my husband had been wounded in the service, so they gave us tickets to go to the program. We wanted to squeeze in everything we could. We went, and we sat through this little mystery. I can close my eyes and see it. We had this program that they were taping, and the mystery was on stage, and they were performing. They were going through the play, and I had my eyes closed because I was trying to visualize the whole scene in my mind — trying to find out who the murderer was. A gun went off, and I think I just jumped. If you knew who the murderer was, you had a chance to win a war bond. They asked me if I knew who the murderer was, and I told them, and I guessed properly, correctly, and I got a war bond. That was just so exciting, because we bought our war bonds and kids at school bought their little stamps. In fact, I even have a book of them yet that I have saved. You put a little twenty-five-cent stamp in the book until it was so filled and they would get a war bond. So I got a war bond, then they mailed it on to me. That was exciting.

We got out of Radio City and we saw servicemen from all over — Russian sailors, and our sailors, and different uniforms. This was exciting to us, because we never were far from home — from Wisconsin to Michigan at that time — so, it was exciting, and we came home. The trains were just jammed with service people, just jammed. I don't know where they were going, but everybody had a place to go to. We came home and then back to the old scene again. Back to work, getting up, going to work, coming home; same old routine.

*   *   *   *   *

Jean Lechnir

At the time the war broke out, the time they took my husband, I had two babies and another one on the way. I got pregnant in February, they took my husband in July, and I didn't have that baby until October. . . . We had no money. I think there was fifty dollars in the bank because he earned about, oh, I would say, fifty dollars every two weeks. Twenty-five dollars a week was all he was earning at the woolen mill at the time. So I gave him the fifty dollars so that he'd have something in his pocket while he was gone, to be inducted and so forth.

He was drafted?

Yes. We even wrote a letter to the draft board and asked them if they would please let him stay home until the baby was born. We never even got the courtesy of an answer from our local draft board, which my husband more or less told them that they could go you know where, and he said, "I'll go."

How did you feel about that?

Terrible — angry, very angry because we had some young men my husband's age that had no children, weren't even married, and their parents had bought them farms or the married ones went out quick and adopted a baby, which didn't even seem to make any difference with me or with my own natural baby. And one of them had an uncle on the draft board, [and] he wasn't even called up for draft. That sort of thing made we women that had our husbands in the service very angry. My husband said he didn't mind going, but he thought everybody that was eligible and had passed the physical should go. I mean, if he had to go, he wanted them all to go with him. . . .

Jean and Ray Lechnir,
Prairie du Chien,
November, 1944.

Courtesy Jean Lechnir. WHi(X3)48319

My husband sneaked home one time, he and his three buddies. They all went in at the same time, and they were supposed to go overseas at New Year's. So Christmas they were given a three-day pass. So they were supposed to go only as far as Schenectady, New York. But the guy that signed their pass, his name started with PD, his initials were PD and his last name started with a C, so the guys took their passes and they covered up the last of his name so it said PDC, Prairie du Chien, PDC, and they got on a train and they came all the way to Prairie du Chien on a three-day pass. The only time they were checked was on the Zephyr coming from Chicago, and this was in the morning and the Zephyr pulled in here around noon, I think, at that time, or close around there, and [the conductor] checked him and he said, "Boy, are they ever lenient with your passes out there. That you can go all the way from New York to Prairie du Chien on a three-day pass." He said, "Be sure you get back." Well, the guys were just sweating blood, you know, and they got home and they stayed overnight and went back. They were home for one whole day, and then they went back that next day.

When my husband knocked on the front door, I was feeding my aunt, uncle, and grandfather with one duck. Now this is a duck, not a goose; this is the kind of Christmas dinner I had. Well, by the time this great big man and his wife, who were both around three hundred pounds, got through with the duck, then my little girls — I mean, they got whatever else was on the table. I don't remember now, but they didn't get any of the duck. My grandfather was late. My husband walked in, all there was [left] was a skeleton and nothing on the table to eat.

After we got through with all the excitement and everything else, I said, "Oh, I haven't got any food in the house." So I had a friend that lived across the street that ran a restaurant, and I knew that she fed all the gentlemen and people that had no permanent home, and they ate with her every day. She always had her back door open at Christmas Day and served those people a free Christmas dinner. So I called her up and I said, "Edie, do you happen to have any food left that I can buy?" I said, "Ray surprised us and I haven't got one stick of food left in the house." She said, "You send that young man right over here." And I said, "Well, he's busy talking." She said, "You come over." And she sent a tray of food you wouldn't believe, and she wouldn't let me [pay], not one dime. She said, "Any boy that's in the service and is going to fight for our [country] — I'm not charging him a nickel." So he had a real good meal. In fact it was awful hard for the rest of us to keep our hands off of it because we hadn't seen food like that for a long time. . . .

My husband was pretty sneaky. Now, when he was going across the Rhine, he told me, "Now, Jean, I can't tell you where I am and what we're doing, but if you're standing on George McClure's front porch" — now, that was a tavern that was on the island over there by the Villa Louis — and he said, "If you're looking west you'll know what I'm going to do." Well, I knew he was going to cross the Rhine because if you're looking west you're going across the Mississippi. He was going across the Rhine. And I followed everything, Bill Mauldin's accounts of what the doughboys were doing, or the dogface, they called him. Well, I followed every article in the papers and stuff like that, and then I cut them out and put them in this scrapbook for him, and then I would put this letter that he sent. A lot of it was cut out, you know, but he got pretty good at writing little hints like that so that they didn't cut out these things, and then I put those all in this scrapbook along with it and it's really amazing how accurate I got on following his march to Germany, whatever. It kept me busy, kept me thinking, and made me feel closer to him.

How did it feel to be apart?

Terrible. When I saw him walk out that back door, and he wouldn't let me go up to the courthouse where they were going to get on the bus to go to Chicago — he wouldn't let me go. Of course I had two little ones in bed and pregnant with another one. It was terrible seeing him walk up this back road here and looking back and I thought, "Oh, here I am with practically three children, and am I going to get him back? What am I going to do if something happens to him?" Those things went through my mind, and he kept saying, "I'm coming back, I'm coming back." . . .

After he was over there for a while he was in a battle and he was wounded and his sergeant was killed right beside him and it made him feel terrible, because he admired his sergeant very much. The funny part is, . . . one of my very good friends, her husband had been in the First World War, just the tail end, and he was a mailman and he did special deliveries. When he found out that maybe Goldie or I or Vi or any of us got a letter from our husband and it wouldn't be delivered till Monday, he'd deliver it on Sunday, just as a special courtesy for us. Well, he brought me this letter Sunday morning, and I was getting ready to go to church, and I opened it up and the first thing he said, "Now, I don't want you to get too excited," he said, "I can walk, I can talk, I can see, and I can hear, and I can feel with my hands, but I have been wounded and I'm in a hospital in France." Well, he said, "and as to how I was wounded, get the *Saturday Evening Post*, such and such an issue, and read that article."

I ripped out the front door. I didn't have a *Saturday Evening Post*, but I knew my neighbor did, and he was 4-F, so I knew they had the *Saturday Evening Post*. I went over and we read it and we got just hysterical, we started to laugh. And I said it's a terrible thing to laugh about your husband being wounded, but in the article it said about the fellow he was in the war and he heard the shell coming in and he dug down into the dirt and forgot to tuck his rear end in, and that's what he got shot. That's exactly what happened to my husband: his derriere got some lead in it. Well, then we got laughing and about two days later I got the telegram from the government that he had been wounded in action. By that time I knew he was all right, that he was hurt and he was in the hospital, but nothing really serious at the time, so the telegram didn't scare me. Now, I was glad that I got the letter before the telegram, or I'd have been a hysterical mess. And his mother lived across the street, too, and she had two sons and three nephews in the service and got them all back, too. But, anyway, we got quite a laugh over that.

Then the local newspaperman came down and he said, "Jean, I've got an article about your husband. I know you'd love to have it." It was written by one of the correspondents out there, and it said, "We interviewed this gentleman from Prairie du Chien, his name is Ray Lechnir, and [he] has a family back there." And they said, "They'd like to know that he's perfectly all right. He can't sit down too well, but the only thing he was mad about was the fact that when the bullet came in, it tore up his canteen and ruined his chocolate candy bar that he was saving out of his kit."

Did he come home soon after that?

The war was over in, let's see, April, 1945, and he came home in September — delay in route. He was supposed to go over into the Pacific, but when they're delay in route they have thirty days off. While he was home, delay in route, they lowered the points. Every man was in there on a point system. You got so many points for age, marriage, children, and so forth — and a wife, of course. There was enough points for him to get out, so he went right up to Tomah and got out of the service, so he didn't have to go over to the Pacific.

I'll bet you were happy about that.

Yeah, we were very happy about that, and then, well, we had a very tough year. Every time if we had a little noise, like if you had a radio on, and you hear a sound like a bullet coming in, if he was sleeping on the davenport he'd roll off the davenport and try to crawl under it. It was just like reminiscent of the war. He couldn't stand the kids [fighting]. Now, see, they were older and fighting like kids will fight and scream and holler and yell and that made him very nervous, very, very nervous. Took him almost a year to adjust to loud noises, cars backfiring, any of that kind of stuff. But I think that's typical of most men that have had an experience [like that].

*   *   *   *   *

Loa Fergot

Born in Neenah in 1924, Loa (Hutchins) Fergot met Paul Fergot in December, 1941, while she was a high school senior. The couple married during the following September, shortly before he left to join the Army Air Corps. Like many other cadet wives, Loa followed her husband as he moved to various training sites throughout the United States during the next two years. Because of her secretarial skills, she easily found work during this period, including a six-month stint with the War Department in Morgantown, West Virginia. When Paul completed his training and went to Europe in August, 1944, Loa returned to Wisconsin, where she worked and attended Oshkosh State Teachers College. Paul, a navigator on a B-24, was shot down over Italy in October, 1944. The army listed him as missing in action until March, 1945, when Loa learned that he was a prisoner-of-war in Germany. The Fergots were reunited in June, 1945, in Milwaukee, and they subsequently settled in Oshkosh. They remain active in civic and ex-POW groups.

Paul first was sent to Miami Beach. What was your impression when you joined him?

When I left [Wisconsin] it was eight below zero and when I got down to Jacksonville, I had to change trains, and I couldn't believe it, it was so warm. And I had never been down South in winter. That was a completely new experience for me and I was so naive in so many, many ways. And it was a new world, but it was an exciting new world. I don't remember that I was particularly afraid, even though I didn't have a place to live and I had almost no money. I spent a lot of time waiting just to see Paul, and we had good help from the churches — both where Paul's parents were, in Oshkosh, and my folks' church in Neenah — in setting up letters of introduction to churches and places down there where they helped us, helped me find places to live. And so I was pretty well protected.

The only thing I really didn't [expect] — I was so naive — was discrimination. We didn't know what it was because my parents treated everybody in the very same way, and they taught us to believe that we were just as good as anybody else in the world, but no better. And it was a wonderful way to grow up. When I was in grade school, there was a black family in Neenah, and they were well-educated and loved, really, and respected very highly. There was never any discrimination that I knew of at that time for them. Later on there was, in the area. I think it was about that time that Marian Anderson tried to stay overnight in Appleton and they wouldn't let her. And my grandmother, who was quite liberal, the one who taught music, was so upset that [even though] she had always been a Republican and she had a [cat named] Hoover, . . . she changed Hoover's name to Roosevelt. . . . So, when I left Oshkosh and Neenah and found the vast amount of discrimination there was in the South, it really [upset me].

Miami Beach, as you know, was separated, Gentiles and Jews. And I couldn't believe that. And I would go down during the day because I had so much time and sit on the beach, and there were so many Jewish people there who couldn't speak English and they would want me to write letters for them. And I would try and interpret what they were saying and put it down and I used to spend a lot of my time in Miami Beach just trying to write letters for them. And, so, you know, that was all new to me, that there was any kind of feeling. . . .

In Montgomery I was riding on a bus one day and I went directly to the back, knowing that it was supposed to be for blacks. There were some blacks sitting back there and the bus driver stopped the bus and he got up and came back and said, "You can't sit back here." And I said, "Why not?" And he said, "Because you have to sit up in front." And I said, "Well, in that case I'll get off the bus." So I got off the bus. But can you imagine being that discriminative? I mean, it was very hard for me to understand it — I just simply couldn't. I knew there were problems, a lot of problems there, but it still was hard for me to understand that whole thing.

I was told in West Virginia, when I got a government job, a civil service job with the War Department, and my best friend there was Jewish and she was a cadet's wife also. And I was called into . . . [a sergeant's] office and told that I was too young to realize it, but I shouldn't be spending so much time with this friend, and that he was sure that my parents would not approve of it. So I told him that my parents would absolutely not care whatsoever one bit about it. They would be very happy if they thought that she was the kind of person that I should be friends with. But anyway, that was all new to me and I learned in a hurry that the world was all black and white, I guess. Or maybe it was white and black — I don't know.

You were in Miami Beach and you had very little money and no place to stay. What did you do?

I found a place because I had a letter of introduction from the minister. I took it to a church there, . . . and so I didn't have a real problem there at all. It was nice. And we had enough money, I guess, when we started out. But there were many times when I tried to find a place, when I would knock on doors. And often, as I told you before, the cadet wives would help each other, so that I would sometimes have a place before I got there. But when I got to Lakeland [Air Corps Base, Florida], I didn't have a room, and I had to knock on doors. And I got into a place that — I didn't stay there terribly long. I think I moved after a week or so, because I would get up [and] turn the light on during the night, and the cockroaches were so big, and I had never seen a cockroach in all my life. They were so huge, and they would run across the floor so fast. And the first night I was there I couldn't sleep and so I finally decided — it was an iron bed — I got my cold cream and I put gobs of cold cream on the legs of the bed, so if they started to climb up the legs of the bed, they [slid down]. And that's what I did as long as I stayed in that place. And then I found another room in Lakeland where it wasn't too bad, so I got over that. But that was the only way I could go to sleep, was to use the cold cream.

But one of the most difficult cities I had to find a place in was Lancaster, California [the future Edwards Air Force Base], which is [in] the Mojave Desert, and here was this huge, huge air base right near there and the town had about five hundred people, I think. And I knocked on doors and knocked on doors and couldn't find a place. And Paul had been told that it would be like that — we knew that, we were aware of it. I spent the first night in a chicken coop, and I think the landlord really took pity on me and said, well, in a day or two, he'd have a place, but if I wanted to sleep in the coop out back, I could. And that's what it was — it was a chicken coop. It didn't have chickens in it, but I was sure it had rats and everything else. And there was an old bunk bed there, and it was in terrible condition. That's where I spent that night, and I didn't sleep much that night, either. There were some nights like that. I think it was the next day that he found me a room. When I look back at some of that, I wonder how I ever had the courage to do all that. Worked out fine.

What was your daily routine in all these different places?

Well, Miami was exciting because it was a whole other world, and it was beautiful and it was warm and it was February and I could go down to the beach. And, as I told you, I just spent the day helping people write letters, and so that wasn't too bad. Well, then, in almost all of the other places, with the exception of Lancaster, once Paul got his commission in Monroe, Louisiana, everything was different. But when he was in training in each place, there were things set up. There were offices set up to help people find housing, or the churches would, or the cadet wives would have something that you could find by going through them. . . .

When I lived with cadet [wives], and usually there'd be four or five in a home, and each one would have a bedroom, and generally, we'd have a kitchen that we could use, which we did. So we spent all our time together, and we really bonded and really had some wonderful friendships. We played cards, we went downtown, we went to movies. We went out to the base whenever we were allowed to,

Courtesy Loa Fergot. WHi(X3)48522

Cadet wives Loa Fergot, Mary Williamson, Adele Robinson, and Gloria Oleshansky, Lakeland, Florida, October, 1943.

which was not very often and usually amounted to about once a week. Our husbands, after a certain length of time, might be able to get off the base on the weekends. But we lived to see them, really. And we had good times together, because we were in such like situations. And I think that we didn't really believe that our husbands would ever go overseas. Not really. We thought the war'd be over before they finished their training, because that's quite a lengthy training. And if we did think about it, we probably just shoved it into the back of our minds, so we had a pretty good time. And in Lakeland, for instance, . . . of the four cadet wives and their husbands, one husband was shot down — after he got his commission — over Europe and was killed. And one was shot down over Germany, became a prisoner-of-war, and died in prison camp. And one was shot down in the Pacific and died. And Paul was the only one who lived, and he became a prisoner. So you can see what the chances were for airmen in those days. They were pretty slim, very slim. I used to know statistics and they weren't encouraging.

Did you know that at that time?

Yes.

*Did you and the other wives ever talk about what you would do when
your husbands went to war?*

I think we did. I think we all had an idea what we would do, pretty
much. But I'm not sure we really believed that time would ever
come, because we kept hoping the war would be over. You see,
when Paul was in Selman Field in Monroe, where he got his commission, I knew that after that he'd be gone. It would be just a matter of a couple of weeks, probably two weeks. And I also knew that
D-Day had come. It came when I was in Monroe, and I remember
D-Day was a very, very important day always to me, because it was
such a great day, to believe that we had actually come to that point
in the war. And I remember Eisenhower [and] a lot of people said,
"The war is going to be over in the fall or before Christmas." Well,
it wasn't, but I think we maybe believed that, I'm pretty sure, so we
thought, "Well, maybe they wouldn't have to go."

Were some times tougher than others for cadet wives?

[Yes]. In many cases, [the cadets] washed out. The percentage of
those who got their wings was really small, really — I mean com-
paratively. And it was tough, it was really tough. And for instance,
Paul took pilot training first and he washed out of that, and that
was very difficult for him and very difficult for me. He then was sent
to Nashville, where he was given tests, and they decided that he
would also make a good navigator. And so, once he got into navi-
gation school, he didn't have any problem, because that was his
field, really. He had problems with flying, and that's why he washed
out.

But it was very difficult for the cadets because they never knew,
sometimes until the very last minute, that they were going to actually finish in a school. One of the things that was most difficult for
me and, I think, [other] cadet wives was that we didn't know when
they were going to be shipped out. We might have some general
idea, but we didn't know when they were going to be sent from one
place to another. We knew that they were going to be sent somewhere, when they finished one place, but . . . we never knew the
day. . . . We didn't know, often, where they were going. So that
was pretty difficult, because it left us kind of in limbo. You know,
we wouldn't know, "Do we go home? What do we do now? Do we
stay here?" In Morgantown, because I had such a good job with the
War Department, I stayed there for about three months after Paul
moved on. . . . The most difficult thing, of course, was when they

did get their commission or wash out, and in many cases when they washed out, they were sent almost immediately overseas into some other area. That was pretty hard on the wives that had that happen.

Tell me about the various jobs that you had while you followed Paul.

Most of them were temporary. I was able to get temporary jobs just by going to the employment agencies. Those were really what I wanted, and so I worked in a lot of different places. In Montgomery, I worked quite a while, actually, for the Montgomery *Alabama Journal*. In Miami Beach I worked for a very short time stuffing envelopes. Somebody had advertised for that and so I did that for a few days. Most of the jobs were of just a few days duration, except that there were some that were longer. Then, of course, the one at the War Department, working for the Morgantown Ordnance. There, I worked for this major who was from the Corps of Engineers. He had been sent there to set up the construction, and he was winding up his job, so that by the time I was ready to leave there and move on, he was about ready to leave, too. The Corps of Engineers had finished its job there. On Thanksgiving Day [1943] I had to leave Lakeland, because Paul was shipped out on Thanksgiving Day, which I didn't know he was going to be. And I came home to Oshkosh and Neenah and I worked at Miles-Kimball in Oshkosh on the night shift from then until after Christmas or whenever that job was finished, because that's a seasonal job. And so I had a lot of jobs like that — I was always able to find something that would help, and we needed the money then.

When you were applying for the Morgantown job, did you know that it would last longer than a few weeks?

Yes, because Paul was at the university there, and I knew that he would be there for three months — that long, at least. And it was a good job, and so I'm sure that that was why I stayed on longer, because at that point, he was going to be moving around quite a bit in the near future. So I stayed there, and at Nashville he was not in any position to have me come there. I went there for a weekend and that was all.

What were the male-female dynamics like at the Morgantown plant, with men and women working so closely together? Was there a problem there?

I don't think so, not a lot of problems. I think every place I worked, there was a certain amount of sexual harassment. But I also felt that

if you let them know that you really didn't want any part of it, it
worked, pretty much.

What sorts of things?

Oh, just hassling, you know, and touching all the time, that sort of
thing. Not putting you down because you were a woman, really. I
don't mean that. I mean attention that you might not want, that's
all. And it wasn't really a problem for me there at all, not in Morgantown. It was [a problem at] a couple of other places where I was
working, and I just left those jobs. That kind of attention was everywhere I'd go, really, because there were so many servicemen where
I'd be. I'd be riding on a train, and . . . there'd be a lot of servicemen on it, and often [the trains] were so crowded that you would
have to sit in the aisles on your suitcases, luggage. And there were
always servicemen who wanted to take you over to their seat or be
especially nice to you, and you had to be concerned because you
didn't know what the next step was going to be. But, all in all, they
treated me pretty well. I didn't have any real problems.

Courtesy Loa Fergot. WHi(X3)48521

Loa Fergot, Lakeland, Florida, fall, 1943.

What was it like to be back in Oshkosh without Paul?

I know I started school, so I kept very, very, very busy. I got a job and started school. I worked part-time as a bookkeeper and went back to school full-time — just so I wouldn't think, I guess. I had a wonderful trip back home. That was beautiful, and I had a Pullman and the lady in the bunk below me was an attorney, a black woman attorney, which for those days was very unusual. And we really got to know each other and enjoyed each other's company all the way home. So I had her to talk to all the way across the country, which was nice. And then, when I got home, I had a lot of people meeting me. And so I think they believed Paul when he said they should keep me busy, so they did. It wasn't easy, but I managed.

What was your reaction to getting mail from Paul?

Well, I guess I lived for the letters, really. I mean, that was the top priority in my day. It was a problem getting letters, because I moved around quite a bit. I'd go to Neenah on weekends and I'd stay with Paul's folks during the week. And sometimes [the letters] wouldn't catch up with me or I wouldn't get them on the day that I wanted to.

That fall they had a difficult time with mail. Some of the servicemen overseas weren't getting their mail at all, and they finally discovered that the reason was that they were sending all these ballots over there for the general election in November. They wanted to make sure every serviceman overseas got a ballot, so he could help elect a president, and they were holding back on other mail. And when they finally realized what was happening, then I guess the servicemen just said they were going to revolt if they didn't get their mail. So they finally changed it in a hurry. And then, after that, until Paul was shot down, the mail was pretty good, the service. But I know I lived for those letters, yes. And then, when there'd be a long period, from the 10th of October, when he was shot down, until the 25th [of October], when I heard he was missing, I got a few letters, but I didn't get many after that. I wrote letters to him all that time, and of course they were all returned, [stamped] missing in action, so . . .

How did you find out that Paul had been shot down and was missing in action?

I got a telegram. It came to Neenah, to my folks' house, and — I don't even know if I can talk about this. I was in school and it was between classes and I was standing by my locker, putting my books in, and I saw my folks walking down the hall. I knew right away what had happened, so — it was really tough, because I just slid down to the floor and sat there for a long time. And, of course, then my dad got down next to me, and he said, "He's only missing, you know, so there's lots of hope yet." So that was the way I was greeted with that.

How hopeful were you?

Well, I think after the shock wore off I was hopeful. I think for a while it was really pretty hard to feel. I went home with my folks to Neenah, and I can remember not wanting to do anything or think or move even. I kind of just sat. But we got very conflicting reports. Got a letter from General [Nathan Farragut] Twining, and he said that . . . they'd seen five or six of the ten parachutes, but that they had bailed out over the Adriatic Sea. That wasn't too hopeful. And then we got another report that somebody said that they had seen them over northern Italy bailing out, and that seemed more hopeful. So you'd kind of go back and forth with all these reports. And we had maybe half a dozen different reports, but none of them was the same, so you didn't really know what to believe. But I think I had a lot of hope then. I think I started to have hope, and I think I did have a lot of hope.

It's kind of hard for me to remember what happened for a while after that. I can't even remember. But I remember staying in Neenah for a while, and then I thought I'd go back to school next semester, so I dropped out of school and stayed in Neenah, and then my dad seemed to think I should be getting a job. So the next thing — this is kind of funny — we were sitting at the table one night and Joseph McCarthy called from Appleton. And he knew my dad, and he said he had just heard that my husband was missing in action and he was just getting out of the Marine Corps, was going to set up his law office in Appleton, and would I come and work for him? And, even back then, my dad, well, he knew [McCarthy], felt that he was probably not the kind of person that I would want to work for. So I didn't, and I didn't want to. I wasn't ready at that point to do anything like that and so I didn't. But I've always thought, over the years, it would have been strange if I had ended up working for Joe McCarthy.

How long did it take for the initial, paralyzing shock to wear off to where you were able to pick up some hope and go through your daily life again?

I don't know. I'm not sure when I started working, but I started working for the Menasha Woodenware, in the office. And they were doing war production. And so I remember walking to work real often because it wasn't too far from where my folks lived in Neenah. And it almost seemed like each day I got more hope and more hope even though I didn't hear anything at all. And none of the crew had been heard from at that point. But then, sometime, I think in February, I got word from the pilot's wife that she had heard that her husband was a prisoner. So I think that gave me the most hope — then I was able to [hope].

And then it wasn't until March that I found out that he was prisoner, and from then on, I can remember, every day was beautiful. I'd walk to work and it would be just gorgeous out, and oh, it felt so good. It was really wonderful, even though I didn't hear from him for a long time, at least I knew that he was a prisoner, and the way I heard was a thrill. . . . I got a telegram from the government [in] which they said that they had intercepted this broadcast, and then I

Courtesy Loa Fergot. WHi(X3)48523
Loa and Paul Fergot, summer, 1945.

got many, many, many — I never did count them, but there must have been close to a hundred — letters, calls, some telegrams, postcards from ham radio operators on the East Coast [of the United States] who had picked up this German propaganda broadcast in which they said that Paul was a prisoner-of-war. And there was a message from him, and so that was the first I really heard. And I was so grateful to all these people, because night after night these people sat and listened to their shortwave broadcasts, and they would write to the people and make sure they had heard, and I thought that was a wonderful thing for those people to be doing.

How did you feel when these postcards started coming in?

Oh, just wonderful. It was a really great time. It's such a thrilling thing to have happen, to have all these people write to you and tell you this. It's just part of that whole united war effort. . . . I don't know, I guess I've always been a believer that adversity brings strength and unity. And I'd hate to think that we have to have terrible things happen to us to bring out the best in people, but I'm afraid sometimes it's true.

Near the end of the war, you knew that the camp had been liberated, but you didn't know what was happening yet with Paul. When did you finally find that out?

The first word I got was from his pilot, I think. He'd seen him, said he was fine. And [the pilot] was able to get to a point where he could send me a telegram, which he did. And then I got another telegram from a friend who had been with Paul in Le Havre, [France,] where they were being rehabilitated, and he told me that Paul was okay. And then I got word from Paul. I got a telegram from him, and then I got letters from him right away from Le Havre, so those were the first real contacts.

What was it like when you first saw him again in Milwaukee?

There are some things you just can't describe, really. . . . It seemed like my life was beginning again.

7

The War Ends

NEWS of Germany's surrender received a quiet welcome in Wisconsin on May 8, 1945. Churches held prayer services and taverns closed, but defense plants continued to operate, with lower than usual absenteeism. Although the war ended in one part of the world, for Americans the job was only half finished. As a Madison woman put it, "I won't do any cheering until it's over in the Pacific because that's where my husband is."

Victory over Japan provoked a wildly different reaction. News of the war's end hit Wisconsin at six o'clock in the evening on Tuesday, August 14, 1945, and celebrations took place throughout the state. In Madison, Milwaukee, Oshkosh, Racine, and in almost every other community, people gravitated to downtown business districts and celebrated for most of the night. The spirit of rejoicing seemed the same, whether in Milwaukee, where a quarter of a million people crowded onto Wisconsin Avenue, or in tiny Mishicot, where crowds went from tavern to tavern drinking toasts and a band of World War I veterans played. People improvised and celebrated in their own style. An all-black swing band quickly set up on Kilbourn Avenue in Milwaukee and their audience started jitterbugging in the street. A Boy Scout drum-and-bugle corps in Madison paraded around the capitol playing "On Wisconsin" and the "Marine Corps Hymn." Many bars around the state closed down, prompting one citizen to complain that it was "a hell of a time to close taverns."

Despite the communal nature of the celebration, the war's end had a deeply personal meaning for most of the citizens of the state. A young woman in Valders hugged a reporter from a nearby Manitowoc paper and told him, "My boy friend is on Iwo Jima — now he will come home and we can get married — ain't it wonderful." A four-year-old boy in Appleton informed everyone who would listen, "My Daddy's coming home." A young mother, with two children holding her hands, walked down a Milwaukee street, her cheeks wet with tears, repeating, "Just think, no more war. No more war."

The end of the war left an idelible impression that remains almost fifty years later. Jean Lechnir, Rose Kaminski, Signe Cooper, Mary Joan Pinard, Loa Fergot, and Dorothy Zmuda all remember vividly how they reacted to the news that peace had at long last returned.

Jean Lechnir (Prairie du Chien)

The word came through on the radio that the war was over in Europe, it was a week and a half or two weeks before it really was over, and I heard it on the radio. I raced out that front door, I tore the screen door right off the front porch and carried it halfway down the yard, running to my neighbor to tell them that the war was over. And the first thing he did was get out a bottle of wine — we had to have a drink of wine. At that time I didn't care whether I had wine or not, but, anyway, we had to have wine and celebrate and everything else, and by that night they said no, that was a false alarm. So then I had to have my neighbor come over and help me hang the door back on the front porch. But then, about two weeks later, the war was over. Of course we had another celebration in the neighborhood, everyone was just whooping and shouting and carrying on. I knew then that our husbands would be coming home, but we didn't have any idea when. You see, when they had the [atomic] bomb went off, and we said, "Good, blast it right off the face of the earth." That was our attitude here. Japan should have been no more, as far as our attitude was concerned, because people never got over it, that Pearl Harbor attack.

Rose Kaminski (Milwaukee)

Well, my husband was home on leave and, . . . I don't know how we heard. . . . But I know word got around [that] it was V-J Day and my husband, naturally, was elated. All the servicemen were. How we got together, I don't know. But I do know that my husband's brother and his wife — he had a car — came over and picked us up and we picked up my sister and her husband and everybody was out in the streets, and shouting, and yelling, and hugging, and kissing each other. We were going to go out and we were going to celebrate because my husband was home on leave — it was cause for celebration. Six of us piled into one car, and we headed for

Milwaukee Sentinel photo.
The celebration of V-J Day on Wisconsin Avenue
in Milwaukee, August 14, 1945.

one of the taverns. We started out in Bay View, where my sister
lived, and we stopped at one of the neighborhood taverns, and it
was just jam packed. Everybody hugging and kissing and buying
drinks for one another. I know I was not a drinker, and my sister
was not a drinker, but we had a drink — I don't know what it
was — beer or what. Then we left and we went to another tavern,
we stopped there, and we had another drink and we were all feeling
pretty happy and real high. I think the adrenaline was not from the
drinks. I think it was from the excitement of the day — the fact that
victory, finally victory. . . . We headed downtown. The nearer you
got to Wisconsin Avenue, the more jammed it was — cars bumper
to bumper. You could not even drive three or four feet, and you'd
stop and people would get out of the cars, hug one another, kiss one
another, yelling and hollering. It was pandemonium. It was just
unbelievable.

Signe Cooper (India)

I don't remember exactly when I heard the news about V-E Day.
But I do remember about V-J Day because I remember when the
corpsman came to say that the war was over. I can remember exactly where I was standing and I said to him, "We have heard this

all week, how do we know this isn't just another rumor?" because there were lots of rumors before the war ended. Before it finally ended there were lots of rumors. He said, "This really is not a rumor, this is really it." And somehow whether he had been sent — like I say, I don't know where the news came in — apparently to go around to all the wards to tell everybody that the war was over.

Mary Joan Pinard (Prairie du Chien)

I was at home pressing a dress to go out for dinner. The young man I had been dating, one of them, was home on leave and we were going out for dinner with some friends of his, and I don't even remember if I finished pressing the dress. The bells started ringing [and] we knew — bells and the whistles and everything. I know that everybody, wherever we went in town, everybody was just wild with elation. You were hugging and kissing everybody that you could see and they [were] jumping up and down. The town was just alive with noise. That's the main thing I remember about it and the elation was there still the next day. People were a little tired. They had pretty much celebrated the night through but then as the days went on, the elation kind of died down into the knowledge that the worst was over but there were still pockets of fighting going on that was going to take a while and that it didn't mean that within two weeks everybody was coming home, that it was going to take a while. But

Mary Joan Pinard,
Prairie du Chien, 1942.

Courtesy Mary Joan Pinard. WHi(X3)48461

at least the big thing was finished and you can now start to plan on things ahead.

Loa Fergot (Oshkosh)

[By the time of] V-J Day, Paul was here. We were home on leave, and everybody turned out in the streets. We went down — one of my best girlfriends' husband had also been a prisoner-of-war and had been wounded also. And she was with us and he was with us that night and she was a Wilson in Oshkosh, and they owned the Wilson Music Company, and so we went into Wilson's and we got drums and we got a tuba and a trombone, which I used to play. We got all these instruments and we had this parade right down Main Street in Oshkosh. And it was just a wonderfully delightful time. And then we tried to find a church that was open, and we couldn't find one. They were all locked up, tighter than a drum, which I've never been able to understand. We finally did find one somewhere.

Dorothy Zmuda (Milwaukee)

Everybody in the office said, "Everybody's going to be downtown in Milwaukee. Everybody's going to run downtown." So of course we were going to go see what's going on, too. . . . So after work we all got on the streetcars. The streetcars were just jammed with people. I can remember one streetcar after another jammed and people, I think, had flags and they were yelling and screaming. Everybody was so happy the war was over. And the streetcar was going down National Avenue, and it come in front of Wood Hospital. . . . But here on the grounds are sitting all these veterans, some without legs, in wheelchairs with their legs covered with a blanket, and they're just sitting there watching us, watching these streetcars of mad people going past, yelling and screaming. Well, when the people spotted them everybody just quieted down and it [was] just flat [silence], and then a couple blocks later they started up again. That I remember; I could never forget that.

Epilogue

THE end of more than three years of global conflict meant a resumption of normal life. Men came back from military service, many women left their jobs outside the home, and couples reunited and began families — in short, people returned to their prewar lives. In economic terms, the end of the war resulted in great prosperity, particularly in comparison to conditions during the Great Depression that had prevailed in the 1930's. The American work force would never be the same, as women assumed a larger part in it than ever before. And the United States became a superpower, assuming a global role unprecedented in its history.

In addition to these societal differences, the war altered Americans on a personal level as well — no one could live through such a time and come out unchanged. *How did the war change your life?*

Emily Koplin (Milwaukee)

I was only seventeen years at the time and I think you matured. I think you learned a lot of responsibility. You realized a lot more than a seventeen-year-old child would have if nothing was happening. I learned a lot about family relationships. I learned a lot about responsibilities, and I think in that way it benefited all of us, and I think because of the war you got a deeper feeling about people, about situations, whether it's friends, family. . . . I always wanted to go to New York and I wanted to become a Rockette, and that was an obsession of mine, and I was a good dancer. . . . I probably could have gone to New York and left it all behind, but I didn't do it, . . . so I never became a Rockette.

Loa Fergot (Oshkosh)

Maybe I'm not as afraid to take risks as a lot of people are. . . . When I was growing up, I can remember [my father] trying to be objective about his children and putting their good qualities and their bad qualities into adjectives, and I thought about that today. One thing he put on both sides of mine was that I was impulsive. And I said, "How can you put that on both sides?" And he said,

139

"Well, because it's good and it's bad, you know. But without it, there's no movement. You have to have this sense of impulsiveness in order to grow and experience new things." And he said that's good, and I believe that, and I think that the war years helped me to find out that you could risk, and you can do things, and life is a lot more interesting because of it. I hope I'm a better person. I don't know. I hope I'm a better person because of it.

Annastasia Batikis (Kenosha)

I think it made me grow up a little faster and become responsible for a lot of things. I had mentioned that my mom passed away when the boys were still in service. Well, I ran our household from the time I was a junior in high school until now; I'm still doing it. So I guess even though — I don't feel I missed any of my childhood, I still did a lot of things, but there were a lot of things that I had to be responsible for a little bit sooner than I would have had to if the war hadn't been on and my mom had not passed away. So from that standpoint the war helped me grow up.

Dorothy Weingrod (Milwaukee)

We were raised at that time to expect certain things — you finished school and maybe you worked for a couple of years and then you got married and then — that was the pattern. The war in some cases accelerated that and in some cases retarded that image. But as far as I was concerned, and most of the people like me, that was how we perceived ourselves. . . . I know there weren't any [women I knew] that saw themselves as being physicians or even [going] into the professional world. I mean we didn't really, at that time, think in terms of making any inroad. We moved along the pattern that our parents did. I wouldn't have [moved to Washington, D.C.]. I probably would have stayed here and either taught school or gotten a job and hopefully ended up getting married. That was the pattern. I don't think I would have had the need to leave the way I did because of the war. All of a sudden there just seemed to be more happening on the outside than what was happening here, and it seemed like this was a time to move in that direction. I don't even know if I thought about it that much; you know, when you're twenty-two, you don't think about it.

Frances Reneau (Beloit)

I cannot say that the war really changed my life in any way. I would say that for myself, you go with the punches. Whatever happened at

Frances Reneau and her son, Thomas, Mother's Day, 1945.

Courtesy Frances Reneau. WHi(X3)48351

that time, we had to accept what we could not change. I do feel that in life, with each experience we go through, we gain something. We have a renewed incentive to move forward and look for a better future. Fortunately, there were more opportunities opened after the war for my people, Afro-Americans. With more job opportunities and increased income, our way of living was improved.

Rose Kaminski (Milwaukee)

I think I became a most self-sufficient person. I know that I had to do a lot of things that I would not maybe have done had there been a man around the house. I was an independent person. If there were windows to be washed and I was up on the third floor, I washed them, hanging right out from the inside of the house, outside. I was not going to say that I couldn't do it. I had the old coal stove. My husband was in the service and the grates had burned out. . . . I ordered a set of new grates because those grates were burned out, but, now, how to put that grate in. I wasn't going to ask my dad to do it. I had an uncle that lived in the same house that I did on the first floor, and I lived on the third floor, [but] I wouldn't ask him to do it. My brother and brother-in-laws were in the service, and John was in the service, and I was going to put them in. I tell you, it took me over four hours. I took the grate out, and if I could take the old grate out I could put the new grate in, and that was all there was to it.

Determination — I don't know if I have that determination anymore. But I did learn how to do a lot of men's work that I would not maybe have done otherwise. I was stubborn — maybe that's the Polish in me. I was determined to do it, and I did it. I think I almost cried when I got through. A sense of satisfaction, a sense of relief, and I did it myself. . . .

I think we women were getting braver right along. We were in a man's world, and I think we resented being told what to do. I think women were told what to do long enough. . . . I remember some of the guys saying to me, "What the hell are you working for?" I said, "It's none of your business. I know what I'm working for." So every month when I get my pension check, I know what I was working for. I feel pretty independent right now. My daughters were brought up to feel independent, too. They are both working. Like grandmother, like mother, like daughter, sent down the line.

Vivian Sekey (Sturgeon Bay)

I think I became a better American as a result of this, going through this with my family, and I wanted peace, oh, I wanted peace so bad. It just never seemed that it was going to come. . . . Oh, I just appreciated my country so much more. You take things for granted. I thought, America, this is wonderful, the most wonderful place to live and I know I'm a better American because of that, because I have so many memories of what we did and so forth. I just am very happy that I lived through that period. I think it's made me a better person, more compassionate person. I think I'm more interesting, and I grew up a lot, grew up a lot. Because when I was a little girl we didn't do the things that the kids do now, and I really grew up in those years when we were in — I had to take over, responsibilities and many sacrifices and so forth. I'm happy for that, but I'm sad for the ones that gave their lives.

Biographies of Interviewees

Born in 1927 in Kaukauna, **Annastasia Batikis** was the youngest of three children of Greek immigrants from Constantinople. Her parents, who moved the family to Racine in 1929, spoke little English and emphasized Greek customs in the home. Batikis's mother died during World War II, leaving her with responsibility for caring for the household. Throughout her childhood, Batikis had a strong interest in athletics, and in the spring of 1945 she tried out for the All-American Girls' Professional Baseball League and won a position on the Racine Belles, playing for one season. She worked as a secretary in the Racine school system from 1945 until 1948, when she enrolled at La Crosse State Teachers College, receiving a B.S. in 1952 and a master's degree in 1960. She taught in the Manitowoc schools from 1952 to 1954 and in the Racine public schools from 1954 until her retirement in 1985. She still lives in Racine with her brother, John.

Rubie (White) Bond was born in Pontotoc, Mississippi, in 1906 and remained there until the First World War, when her parents, seeking economic opportunities unavailable to blacks in the South, moved their family to Beloit. Bond attended Beloit College, noted for its willingness to accept black students. In 1928 she married Franklin M. Bond and became a mother to his three daughters from a previous marriage. The Bonds subsequently had six additional children, five of whom were born before World War II started. Her husband died in 1985, and she still resides in Beloit.

Grace (Peck) Bracker was born in Hazelton, Iowa, in 1911 and grew up in numerous small Iowa towns. She received an education degree from the University of Dubuque in 1931 and taught school in Iowa until she married Bernhard Bracker in 1939. The couple subsequently moved to Madison, where she worked as a part-time cook and housekeeper for her landlord. When Bracker was pregnant with her first child, in 1942, she and her husband moved to Edgerton, southeast of Madison, where they remained for the duration of the war. After living in New Mexico from April to December, 1950, the Brackers settled permanently in Madison, where

143

Grace taught in the public school system from 1953 until her retirement in 1977. Her husband died in 1965.

Born in Clinton County, Iowa, in 1921, **Signe (Skott) Cooper** moved with her family to McFarland, just outside Madison, in 1937. Cooper was graduated from the University of Wisconsin's nursing school in 1943. She joined the Army Nurse Corps in May, 1943, and was stationed at Fort Belvoir in northern Virginia, just outside of the District of Columbia, from May, 1943, to August, 1944, when she was sent to the China-Burma-India (CBI) theater. There, she worked in a hospital on the Ledo Road, a route running from Ledo, in the Indian province of Assam, through Burma into southern China. She spent the duration of the war in India, moving to Burma for a month after the war ended. After her discharge at the end of 1945, she returned to Madison, where she worked at Wisconsin General Hospital (now the University of Wisconsin Hospital) and later became a professor of nursing. She retired in 1983 and now lives in the Madison suburb of Middleton.

Born in 1920, **Judy Geraldine (Schamens) Davenport** grew up in Leon, near Sparta, and joined the WAACs in November, 1942. She completed basic training in Des Moines, Iowa, and later was stationed in Georgia and Louisiana as a cook. Davenport served for ten months, choosing not to reenlist because of an injury when the WAAC was converted into the WAC in 1943. She returned to Leon, where she married career military officer James Davenport on October 31, 1944. She spent the next four decades raising the couple's four children and doing volunteer work, primarily in the Leon area. Widowed in 1986, she now lives in Sparta.

Born in Madison in 1916 to Sicilian immigrants, **Anne (Aparatore) Dinsmore** was graduated from the University of Wisconsin in 1938 with a degree in social work. She worked for several years with the Girl Scouts of America in Omaha, Nebraska, but at the start of World War II, she returned to Madison to be with her family. She married in 1943 and gave birth to a son in 1944, after her husband left to serve in the war. The couple later divorced, and in 1966 she joined the Peace Corps, spending two years in South America. After she returned to the United States, Anne remarried and lived for the next several years in the Middle East, primarily in Saudi Arabia. She is divorced and still lives in Madison.

Born in Neenah in 1924, **Loa (Hutchins) Fergot** met Paul Fergot in December, 1941, while she was a high school senior. The couple married during the following September, shortly before he left to join the Army Air Corps. Like many other cadet wives, Loa followed her husband as he moved to various training sites throughout the United States during the next two years. Because of her secretarial skills, she easily found work during this period, including a six-month stint with the War Department in Morgantown, West Virginia. When Paul completed his training and went to Europe in August, 1944, Loa returned to Wisconsin, where she worked and attended Oshkosh State Teachers College. Paul, a navigator on a B-24, was shot down over Italy in October, 1944. The army listed him as missing in action until March, 1945, when Loa learned that he was a prisoner-of-war in Germany. The Fergots were reunited in June, 1945, in Milwaukee, and they subsequently settled in Oshkosh. They remain active in civic and ex-POW groups.

Born in Waunakee, near Madison, in 1913, **Evelyn (Bailey) Gotzion** grew up in Madison and married Steven Gotzion in 1931. The couple had three children, born in 1932, 1933, and 1940. In 1935, Gotzion began work at Rayovac, a manufacturer of batteries and lighting products, and remained there for the next forty-three years, actively participating in union activities. She was widowed in 1975 and continues to reside in Madison.

Eugenia ("Gene") (Amrhein) Gutkowski was born in Milwaukee in 1927 to Catholics of German descent. She left high school in 1943 to help her family financially when her brother left for military service, working at Steinmeyer's Grocery Store until the late 1940's. She then worked at Sealtest Dairy until her marriage to Alfred Gutkowski in 1953. Since that time she has been a homemaker, and she still lives in Milwaukee with her husband.

Born in Wausau in 1917 and raised in Merrill, **Jane Heinemann** received a bachelor's degree in music education from Northwestern University in 1940 and taught music in schools in Earlville, Illinois, and Hammond, Indiana. She joined the Red Cross in 1943 and was sent to Camp Chaffee, Arkansas, an armored training post, where she became a staff recreation worker, charged with entertaining recovering GIs in the station hospital. The Red Cross sent her to the western Pacific in 1945. She first went to Tinian, in the Mariana Islands, with one of five hospitals to be set up for the planned invasion of Japan. Heinemann remained overseas after the war ended and moved to club service on Guam and Saipan. She returned to the United States in early 1946, but later that year the Red Cross coalled her back to William Beaumont General Hospital, in El Paso, Texas, where she worked with long-term battle casualties. She returned to teaching in Michigan, Wisconsin, Illinois, Arizona, Maryland, and Iowa over the next five years before joining the U.S. Army's Special Services and becoming a program director in GI service clubs in Germany during 1953 and 1954. She returned to Wisconsin in 1954 and taught music at the University of Wisconsin-Milwaukee until her retirement in 1986. She now resides in the Milwaukee suburb of Glendale.

Born to Polish immigrants in Kenosha in 1918, **Rose (Gudynowski) Kaminski** moved to Milwaukee at age ten. She married John Kaminski in 1937 and has two daughters, one born in 1941 and the second in 1948. Her husband was drafted in early 1944 and served on a minesweeper in the navy. Beginning in early 1943, she worked in the machine shop of the General Electric Supercharger plant. After about four months there, she became a crane operator for the Rex Chain Belt Company, and in February, 1944, she obtained a similar position with Harnischfeger Corporation, remaining there until March, 1946, when she was released from her job to accommodate a returning veteran. She returned to Harnischfeger in 1950, working there until she retired in February, 1981. Widowed in November, 1988, Kaminski still lives on Milwaukee's south side.

Dorothy (Doxtator) Keating, a full-blooded Oneida Indian, was born in Laona, in Forest County, in 1924. She grew up in a series of foster homes and government boarding schools. Keating joined her mother in Milwaukee in the summer of 1942, after her junior year of high school. Rather than returning to school, Keating got a job making circuit breakers at Cutler-Hammer and later worked at Allis-Chalmers as a coil winder. She joined the WAVES in 1944 and served as a pharmacist mate, second class, for two and a half years, working in Maryland, Oklahoma, and New York. Keating has been married three times, most recently to Thomas Keating, who died in 1990. She worked for the Stockbridge-Munsee Indian tribe for almost ten years until her retirement in 1990, and she earned her high school general equivalency diploma in 1982. She received an associate degree in social work from the University of Wisconsin-Stevens Point in 1985. She currently lives on the Stockbridge-Munsee Reservation, in Shawano County.

Born in 1917 in Rhinelander, **Margaret (Ebert) Kelk** grew up in Lake Tomahawk, where her parents operated a girls' camp. She received a degree in education from the University of Wisconsin in 1939. During her last two years of college, she worked part-time for the *Wisconsin State Journal*, moving to full-time work in the advertising department after graduating. Following the attack on Pearl Harbor, she took a secretarial position with the Badger Ordnance plant in Baraboo, where she worked until she joined the American Red Cross Military Welfare Service in September, 1943. Kelk received two weeks of training in Washington, D.C., before being shipped to the Pacific theater, where she served in New Caledonia, Guadalcanal, and Hawaii. Her only brother, Mark Johnson Ebert, who was eighteen months her junior, was killed on a bombing mission over Bucharest, Romania, on April 4, 1944. After the war, she returned to Wisconsin, where she taught English and social studies at the junior high level at several Wisconsin schools from 1946 until her marriage to Harry Kelk in 1955. Since that time, she has owned and operated a summer campground trailer park in Lake Tomahawk. Her husband died in 1988.

Born in Milwaukee in 1926, **Emily Koplin** grew up in an ethnically diverse neighborhood on Milwaukee's south side. Koplin's father was of German descent; her mother was of French descent and grew up in Canada. Koplin has worked in the office at the Allen-Bradley Company since graduating from high school in 1943, and at age sixty-seven she continues to postpone retirement.

Irene (Cavanaugh) Kruck was born on a farm in Maple Grove, in Manitowoc County, in 1902. After her graduation from high school, she earned her teaching certificate from Manitowoc Teachers College. She taught elementary school in Manitowoc County (1921-27) and then did part-time office work (1927-33). She married Ernest Kruck in 1932 and gave birth to two sons prior to the outbreak of World War II. In 1943, she returned to work in a clerical capacity at the Manitowoc Shipbuilding Company because of the desperate need for workers at the shipyards. Although she had planned to quit when the war ended, she worked until 1982, when she retired. Her husband died in 1964, and she still lives in Manitowoc.

Jean (Hahn) Lechnir was born in 1917 in Prairie du Chien and has lived there her entire life. She received a B.S. degree from La Crosse State Teachers College before marrying Ray Lechnir in 1940. The Lechnirs had two small children and Jean was pregnant with a third when her husband was drafted for military duty in 1944 and sent to Europe, where he served until 1945. The Lechnirs later had three more children, and when their youngest child entered school in the early 1960's, Jean returned to work, holding a variety of jobs until her retirement in 1978. Her husband died in 1981.

Although born in Sheboygan in 1925, **Marjorie Miley** has lived most of her life in Manitowoc, on the Lake Michigan shore. After graduating from high school in 1943, she took a job as a proofreader at the Manitowoc *Herald Times* (later the *Herald Times Reporter*). She spent her entire career with the newspaper, eventually rising to become its managing editor, the first and only woman to serve in that post.

Born in 1924 in Lafayette, Indiana, **Mary Joan (Hammel) Pinard** moved to Prairie du Chien with her mother and her brother in 1932 and has lived in that Mississippi River community since that time. After her high school graduation, Pinard worked at her stepfather's grocery store and then obtained a job at the county clerk's office. During the war, Pinard's brother and father served in the military, and she volunteered her time performing clerical duties for the area scrap-metal drive. She married Paul Pinard in 1948 and raised their two children before returning to work as a clerk and secretary from 1962 until 1981.

The daughter of Lakota Indian and French parents, **Lucille (LeBeau) Rabideaux** was born in Dewey County, South Dakota, in 1914. She attended Indian schools before enrolling in the Sioux City Methodist Hospital Nurses School, from which she was graduated in 1938. Rabideaux moved to Wisconsin in 1939 and worked as a nurse for the Indian Service in Hayward, in Sawyer County. While there, she met Francis Martin Rabideaux, a Red Cliff Chippewa from Bayfield, on Lake Superior. They married in 1941, shortly after he was drafted into the army. In June, 1943, Rabideaux enlisted as an army nurse with the Forty-fourth General Hospital Unit, based from Madison, and she served in Australia, New Guinea, and the Philippines before being discharged in March, 1946. After the war, Francis Rabideaux reenlisted in the army, and the Rabideaux family followed him to a number of posts in the United States and abroad before his death in Thailand in 1968. Lucille Rabideaux then returned to Ashland, where she still lives, and worked as a nurse until her retirement in 1980.

Born in Corydon, Indiana, in 1914, **Frances (Brown) Reneau** spent most of her childhood in Aurora, Illinois. She married Jesse B. Reneau in 1938 and moved to Beloit, where her husband was a Ford mechanic. She worked as a seamstress, first part-time for a local dress shop and later at home, for more than forty years. Reneau took an active part in the civil rights movement in the 1950s and 1960s and remains active in volunteer organizations in the Beloit area. She was widowed in 1987.

Born in Rhinelander in 1917, **Luida Sanders** grew up in a series of towns in northern Wisconsin, including Lake Tomahawk, Wittenberg, West De Pere, and Styles Junction. After graduating from high school in 1934, Sanders worked for part of one year in Racine and for two years at the courthouse in Shawano to save enough money to continue her education. She received a two-year rural teaching certificate from Stevens Point State Teachers College in 1939 and then spent four years as a rural schoolteacher, in Brown and Shawano counties. In 1943, as soon as she could get out of her teaching contract, she joined the Women's Auxiliary Army Corps (WAAC), which later became the Women's Army Corps (WAC), rising to the rank of technical sergeant. She served as a recruitment officer, secretary, and hospital worker and was stationed in Massachusetts, Alabama, and Georgia. After her discharge from the service in 1946, Sanders used the GI Bill to obtain a bachelor's degree in education from the University of Wisconsin. She later obtained a master's degree in public administration from the UW and a master's degree in public health from the University of California at Berkeley. Since the war, she has pursued a career in public health in Wisconsin, and she currently resides in Oshkosh.

Born in 1914 in Lorain, Ohio, to Jewish immigrants from eastern Europe, **Eleanor (Shiff) Schiff** was graduated from Ohio State University in 1938. She married Philip Schiff later that year, and the couple moved to Clarksburg, West Virginia, in January, 1939. They had a son in 1940, a daughter in 1943, and another son seven years later. Shortly after the attack on Pearl Harbor, the Schiffs moved to the Milwaukee suburb of Shorewood, where Eleanor continues to reside. Following her husband's death in 1963, Eleanor opened a travel agency, which she ran until 1988. She remains active in a number of civic and charitable causes.

Born in Tomah in 1921, **Geraldine (Sowle) Schlosser** received her undergraduate education at Milwaukee State Teachers College and the University of Wisconsin. In early 1943, she joined the WAAC, reenlisting in July in the WAC when the WAAC was disbanded. After basic training she attended radio school in Newark, New Jersey, and then served as a radio technician in Midland, Texas, until November, 1945. After the war, she returned to the University of Wisconsin, where she pursued a graduate degree in anthropology and met her future husband, James Schlosser. The couple married in 1947, and the Schlossers moved to Milwaukee, where Geraldine did general office work until the birth of her first child, in 1952. She returned to work in 1960 as an interviewer for the University of Wisconsin Survey Research Laboratory and then attended library school a few years later, receiving her master's degree from the University of Wisconsin-Milwaukee in 1968. She was then employed as a librarian at the Milwaukee Public Library until she and her husband retired and moved to Tomah in 1982.

Born to Swiss immigrants in Dodgeville in 1919, **Frieda Schurch** grew up on the family's farm in Barneveld, in southwestern Wisconsin. After graduating from high school, she attended the University of Wisconsin in 1938-1939 but then returned home to help care for her ailing mother. Following her mother's death in September, 1940, Schurch served as housekeeper for the family's large farm until she joined the WAAC in January, 1943. She remained in the service during the transition to the WAC and was stationed primarily in Des Moines, Iowa, Denton, Texas, and Tampa, Florida, until her discharge in December, 1945. She returned to school, receiving a degree in early childhood development from the University of Wisconsin in 1950, and taught kindergarten in Kenosha from 1952 until 1984. She remains active in politics and still lives in Kenosha.

Vivian (Tronson) Sekey grew up in Forestville, Door County, where she was born in 1916. She received a bachelor's degree in education from Oshkosh State Teachers College and taught elementary school in Door County. In 1942, she married Jesse Sekey, a shipyard worker in Sturgeon Bay. She stopped teaching from the time of her marriage until the birth of her son in 1943 but returned to the classroom because of the shortage of teachers in the area. Sekey taught kindergarten in the Sturgeon Bay public schools until 1979, and she continued as a substitute teacher until 1990. She is a widow and remains active in the Moravian church.

Born to Armenian immigrants in 1924 in Racine, **Rose (Arakelian) Truckey** was originally named Nazeli, but her father changed her name to Rose because a grade school teacher could not spell or pronounce the more traditional Armenian name. During World War II, Truckey got a job at the J. I. Case Company in Racine, working as a riveter on a production line that manufactured bomb bay doors for aircraft. While working at Case, she met Sy Truckey, who was on medical leave from the army. They married in June, 1944, and moved briefly to Rockford, Illinois. When her husband was again shipped overseas, Truckey, who had become pregnant, returned to Racine and found a job at Zahn's Department Store. Following the war, Truckey worked in a Racine bank and advanced as far as vice-president prior to her retirement in 1992. A widow since 1968, she still lives in Racine and was chosen as Ms. Senior Wisconsin in 1990. She has also served on Governor Tommy Thompson's Committee on Aging and on the Salvation Army Advisory Board, and she is a past president of the Point West Business and Professional group.

Lucy Veltri was born in Racine in 1927, the daughter of Italian immigrants. After completing high school, she became a member of the Catholic USO in Racine. Married in 1949, Veltri is the mother of two children. She received a degree in education from Dominican College in Racine in 1974 and taught school until her retirement in 1981. From 1990 to 1992, she served as president of the Racine Area Retired Educators.

The daughter of Jewish immigrants from Poland, **Dorothy (Tuchman) Weingrod** was born in 1921 in Milwaukee. In 1943, several months after her graduation from Milwaukee State Teachers College, she moved to Washington, D.C., where she worked for army intelligence as a private secretary to a captain. She returned to Milwaukee in December, 1945, and in April, 1946, she married Murray Weingrod, who had been in the service, stationed in Africa. Her husband passed away in 1990, and Weingrod, a homemaker and volunteer worker, now lives in Mequon, outside of Milwaukee.

Joyce (Hill) Westerman was born in 1925 in Kenosha, where she was raised on a farm. After graduating from high school, she worked for American Motors in Kenosha until 1944, when she joined the All-American Girls' Professional Baseball League. Westerman played catcher with four different teams in the league from 1945 to 1952 and worked a wide variety of jobs during the off season. She married Ray Westerman in 1950 and returned to work at American Motors from 1951 until the birth of their first child in 1955. She worked as a clerk for the U.S. Postal Service from 1964 until her retirement in 1986. The Westermans still live in Kenosha.

Born in Stevens Point in 1923, **Dorothy (Roshak) Zmuda** moved to Milwaukee in 1942, where she worked at Allis-Chalmers as an advertising layout artist. She returned to Stevens Point in 1945 and married George Zmuda the following year. She worked as a secretary and as a clerk until the birth of the first of their five children, in 1948. Since that time she has been a homemaker and artist. The Zmudas still reside in Stevens Point.

Suggestions for Further Reading
and Location of Original Materials

The last decade has seen the publication of a substantial number of interesting books on the history of women during World War II. The following is a highly selective list of suggestions for further reading.

Susan M. Hartmann, *The Home Front and Beyond: American Women in the 1940s* (Boston, 1982) and D'Ann Campbell, *Women at War with America: Private Lives in a Patriotic Era* (Cambridge, Mass., 1984) have been valuable for drafting the introduction and headnotes to this volume. Hartmann offers a series of topically arranged chapters that summarize much of the recent literature on women during World War II and the postwar era. Campbell stresses continuity over change in women's wartime experiences and presents a wealth of information in an interesting fashion. Karen Anderson, *Wartime Women: Sex Roles, Family Relations, and the Status of Women in World War II* (Westport, Conn., 1981) centers on women's role in three defense communities: Baltimore, Detroit, and Seattle. Maureen Honey, *Creating Rosie the Riveter: Class, Gender, and Propaganda during World War II* (Amherst, 1984) examines the depiction of women in advertising and popular literature during the war. Leila Rupp, *Mobilizing Women for War: German and American Propaganda, 1939-1945* (Princeton, 1978) compares government efforts in both countries to involve women in the war effort.

Readers who wish to understand women's wartime experiences in the context of Wisconsin's history should consult William F. Thompson, *The History of Wisconsin. Volume VI: Continuity and Change, 1940-1965* (Madison, 1988). Wartime letters written by Signe Cooper, Margaret (Ebert) Kelk, and Luida Sanders, as well as others, can be found in Michael E. Stevens, Sean P. Adams, and

152

Ellen D. Goldlust, eds., *Letters from the Front, 1898-1945* (Madison, 1992), in the *Voices of the Wisconsin Past* series.

*   *   *   *   *

All interviews are taken from the Wisconsin during World War II Oral History Project. The original recordings and full transcripts are deposited in the archives of the State Historical Society of Wisconsin and may be used by researchers upon request. Photographs identified with WHi negative numbers are taken from the Society's collections.

Index